LOVE IS A VERB

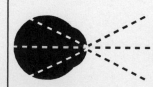

This Large Print Book carries the
Seal of Approval of N.A.V.H.

LOVE IS A VERB

GARY CHAPMAN

THORNDIKE PRESS
A part of Gale, Cengage Learning

GALE
CENGAGE Learning·

Detroit • New York • San Francisco • New Haven, Conn • Waterville, Maine • London

LIBRARY OF CONGRESS CATALOGING-IN-PUBLICATION DATA

Chapman, Gary D., 1938–
   Love is a verb / by Gary Chapman. — Large print ed.
     p. cm.
   ISBN-13: 978-1-4104-1952-1 (hardcover : lg. print : alk. paper)
   ISBN-10: 1-4104-1952-5 (hardcover : lg. print : alk. paper)
   ISBN-13: 978-1-59415-301-3 (softcover : lg. print : alk. paper)
   ISBN-10: 1-59415-301-9 (softcover : lg. print : alk. paper)
   1. Love. 2. Love—Religious aspects—Christianity. 3. Interpersonal relations. 4. Large type books. I. Title.
BF575.L8C44 2009b
177'.7—dc22   2009022279

Published in 2009 by arrangement with Bethany House Publishers.

Printed in the United States of America
1 2 3 4 5 6 7 13 12 11 10 09

Dedicated to

Derek and Amy Chapman,

whose lifestyle demonstrates
that "love is a verb."

ACKNOWLEDGMENTS

I am indebted to those individuals who shared their stories of love with me. This book would not have been possible without their contributions. I am extremely grateful to Jim Bell, who encouraged this project from the beginning and played the major role in collecting the stories. I hope that both he and the contributors will be rewarded by knowing that their work has helped others discover that love is a verb. I'm also grateful to others on the editorial and marketing side who played a role — Kyle Duncan, Tim Peterson, Julie Smith, Ellen Chalifoux, Donna Carpenter, and Jeanette Littleton.

On the personal side, I have been greatly blessed with a son, Derek, and a daughter-in-law, Amy, who have for all of their married lives provided a model of what it means to love. Beginning with their wedding in Prague and continuing with their ministry in Antwerp, and now in Austin, Texas, they have been involved daily in giving their lives away to others. I dream of a day when their example will be multiplied, and to that end I have dedicated this book to them.

Gary D. Chapman
Winston-Salem, North Carolina

CONTENTS

9

11

INTRODUCTION

"Love makes the world go round."

"All you need is love."

"Love can make you crazy. . . ."

As long as any of us can remember, poems, songs, films, and orators have tried to adequately describe and express love. Movies and TV programs focus on the pursuit of love and personal fulfillment. Advertisements use this strong sentiment to sell us products. Our culture often seems to have a love-tracked mind.

Whether it's in marriage, family, or friendships, it's no wonder that love is such a draw and places so high on the priority list in our lives. After all, the wisest book I've ever read, the Bible, tells us that God himself is love.

Few emotions in life equal the exciting adrenaline rush of a newfound romance or the sweet companionship of a friend or the faithful support of a family member. No wonder we seek love above so many other positive experiences. The normal, everyday challenges are so much easier to survive when we know we have people who are always there when we need them and support us unconditionally.

Because every love relationship involves fallible humans, challenges abound. Unlike the personal connections portrayed on the big and small screens, the real issues between people usually can't be resolved within thirty minutes or even a few episodes. Sometimes circumstances and people make it almost impossible to love successfully.

The euphoria subsides after marriage, and the romantic feelings might fly out the window. We have a sharp disagreement and find ourselves being antagonistic instead of supportive.

Sometimes communication quandaries occur. At other times, we may cling to unrealistic expectations. And at other times, frankly, we may not even actually know how love factors into the equation. And when the going gets tough, some people just get going . . . leaving a trail of wounded hearts behind.

As a pastor and counselor, I've seen it over and over again. A spouse gets bored with marriage and gives in to the temptation to see if the grass really is greener in another person's yard. Parents and children emotionally excommunicate each other over a misunderstanding. Someone sits alone at church or stays home because he or she has lost a friend and is afraid to become vulnerable and reach out again.

I've seen too many people give up on love too fast. Walking away from relationships doesn't provide the hoped-for relief, bring solutions, or simplify life. Rather, it piles on more problems through the lingering resentment and finger-pointing.

So what are the answers to the challenges love brings? For starters, to last for the long haul and through the stresses and complexities of life, love has to be more than something we feel. It has to be something we do. We have to demonstrate it concretely in our marriage, our family, among our friends and acquaintances, and, yes, even among our enemies.

And that's what this book is about. In the following pages, you'll see examples of people just like you — like *all* of us — who learned to take the obstacles, the "lemons" they face in life, and turn them into satisfying, emotional-thirst-quenching nectar. These are the success stories that make you want to go out and try harder.

You'll read about:

- Doris, who kept her hands busy furiously knitting when she almost felt like using them to strangle the husband she truly couldn't stand any longer.
- Faith and Louise, who both had to learn how to cope when a stranger's mind inhabited their loved one's body.
- Sarah, who wanted nothing to do with her sisters; and Laquita, who finally fell in love with her husband after forty years.
- Kevin, who found out what sacrifice for another person *isn't* . . . as well as what it *is.*
- Sudha, who literally had a suicidal stranger plopped on her doorstep; and Laurie, who found love peeking through her hedges.
- Steven, who gave a cup of hot coffee to warm the love circulation in his heart; and Tamara, who learned that she had the power to enhance a less fortunate person's world.
- Rebecca, whose father was incapable of showing emotion; and Eileen, who was expressing her emotions way too vividly!
- Midge, the woman who expected

chocolate and ended up with a bitter taste in her mouth.

- Loretta, who crawled through the unbelievable pain of criminal behavior, as she was asked to disinherit a beloved perpetrator.
- Pamela, who ended up finding the treasure of her heart beneath the lid of a small silver box.

All of these people, and a couple of dozen more, share their tales of learning to live out love through tragedy and triumph. Their experiences are more mesmerizing than any contrived Hollywood chronicles could be. You'll be able to connect with their narratives and relate to their angst and achievements.

And after each story, I've highlighted a key element that can help you become unbeatable in your quest for strong, stable relationships. Through these pages, I'll give you practical pointers these people used that you can also put into action. These stories will inspire you to build, rekindle, and experience the kind of love and friendship that endures after the warm fuzzy feelings have faded.

So do you want to enjoy the best relationships possible? Then get to work. Love isn't wrapped up in a pronoun — in "he," "she," or "them." It's not about who other people are or how they treat us or what they do to make us value them. It begins with you, and it's not primarily about what you say or feel. Instead, love is an action word; it's a choice you have to make. *Love is a verb!*

— *Gary Chapman*

LOVING LAVISHLY

Tony walked into our office one day where my husband, Tim, counsels disabled veterans. His brilliant smile lit up his face. He was no taller than my fourteen-year-old — bald, rail thin, and in his late forties. He was so charming, the kind of charm that I'm sure his mother couldn't resist even if he'd been bad. He had this laugh, a half giggle that came so easily I almost laughed too — I couldn't help it. I met him only briefly but he left an imprint on my heart that I didn't even realize was there.

Later that week Tim asked me, "Do you remember Tony?"

"Sure," I said, as I sorted mail.

"Let me tell you a little more about him. He has HIV, is a Katrina refugee, was relocated here to Denver, and from what I can tell he's completely alone. He's been homeless but recently found subsidized housing. However, he's pretty sick, his apartment is basically empty, and he's sleeping on the floor. He doesn't even have a bed."

He doesn't even have a bed — no bed, and he's sick. The words echoed through my mind. *No bed, no bed.* I pictured little Tony curled up on the floor. I've heard of desperate situations like this before, like we all do, and it always grips my heart and I feel terrible. But this time it was like someone shook me and yelled, "He doesn't have a bed! Look at all you have!"

Our family has always enjoyed helping the less fortunate — Christmas gifts to people in hardship, bringing meals to families with someone in the hospital, money to a child in Africa. But those were "safe" ways to help, and then go home; our lives had never intertwined with them.

My stomach tilted and I felt a little shaky. I had to get him a bed. I don't know why this time I had to act, but God knew. And it had to be a new bed! For some reason, I wanted to love him *lavishly.* But even as I felt so driven to help him, I wondered what I was getting myself into. I'd never done anything like this before.

We delivered his bed and brand-new bedding that my girls and I had picked out. I was pretty nervous. He sat on his new bed, smoothed out the covers, and smiled. Then emotion overcame him and he sobbed. Coughs wracked his thin body.

"Thank you. Thank you so much — I don't know what to say. I . . . I . . ." His words drowned in the tears. This bed seemed to be a light in a very dark, deep pit. He looked at us with something like grateful confusion. I don't know how else to describe it. He didn't know us at all.

"Tony, dear! What's goin' on in here?" Juanita, his grandmotherly neighbor from across the hall, walked in. "I'm sure not lookin' right to meet new folks, but I wanted to see what's goin' on!"

She saw his bed and looked at Tony, shook her graying head, and said, "Honey, I told you God would take care of you. He heard you; yes, He did."

Our friends and family jumped right in — new pots and pans, dishes, towels, microwave, money — you name it! And to top it off, my sister Laurie bought him all-new furniture — not everyone's throw-aways, but brand-new, matching furniture with a matching rug.

"Laurie," I said, "I'm kind of nervous about your spending this much money. We don't really know him and he could sell it or someone could steal it or . . ."

"I want to do this, and whatever happens, happens," she said with a smile. Lavish love.

I called one day to check on him. He always had a positive twist on everything. "Well, I'm pretty good, pretty good today. Did you know tomorrow is my birthday?"

"Tony, let's have a birthday party!" My family came, along with my parents and even my daughter's friend. We wrapped the remaining things people had given in colorful bags and brought a cake. He sat on the couch sandwiched between my parents, and the tears flowed. "I've never had a party like this before! I'm one of fourteen kids, you know."

I had no idea. Where was his family? Little slices of his life started to tumble out.

As we drove home, my daughter's friend smiled as she looked out the window and said, "That was the best day ever." When I returned later to take him some food, he had stapled all the gift bags onto his wall.

Tony started to get sicker. He had a lot of chest pain and difficulty breathing. I called to check on him one Monday morning. "I've been in the hospital three times this weekend, Tamara. I had terrible chest pain."

"Oh, Tony!" I felt terrible. "How did you get there?"

"I took the bus, but I had to walk a mile

to the bus stop. They said they couldn't find anything so they sent me home, but I wasn't any better so I went back two more times."

They never even helped him get home! I was livid! In my world, I had family to take me, and a car, and they never would have sent me home like that. In his world he was alone, and they didn't care.

I realized he needed a medical advocate, so Tim and I decided to step in. Perhaps because of his history, perhaps because he was alone, he continued to be treated as if he were not worth the medical professionals' respect or effort. He was hospitalized over and over, and I can't tell you how many times I roared to the hospital when I heard how he was treated. The nurses would ask, "And who are you?"

I'd act offended and say, "Well, his big sister, of course! Can't you see the resemblance?" He's black and 5'6" and I'm white and 5'10".

Tony got worse. I sat with him as he waited to see an oncologist one day. Tony was scared. He turned to me and said, "Why are you doing this? You don't really know me and the things I've done."

I smiled and said, "Well, you don't really know me and the things *I've* done."

"No, really," he urged.

"I think I just happened to be listening to God, Tony. He knew you needed someone to walk beside you right now and just love you."

Tony had lung cancer. We didn't know how much time he had left, and my sister felt an urgency to reunite him with his family. We urged him to call his mom. She lived in Mississippi.

"Oh, I don't want to worry her. She's almost eighty," he said. But wistfulness edged his voice. That was the first we'd heard of his mother, Lucille.

My parents started to visit him at his apartment and at the hospital. He called them momma and papa, and he often cried when he talked to them on the phone. I think he missed his own momma so much.

One night around eight o'clock he called from the hospital. "The doctor is here and . . ." His voice cracked and my throat constricted as he said, "It's not so good, big sister."

He tried to laugh, but it turned to sobs. The doctor took the phone and told me, without emotion, that Tony had stage-four lung cancer, and maybe six weeks to four months to live. I was so angry I was shaking. I had asked the people at the hospital to call me so I could be with him when they gave him the prognosis. To be told such news all alone is even more devastating.

We rushed to the hospital. To my surprise, Tony smiled, held my hands, and this time the tables were turned — he comforted me! I cried and cried.

"I know you think that doctor is mean, but I needed to hear the truth, and no one would tell me," he said.

I realized then how much I really loved Tony.

Tony told me later that after he'd gotten that news he left his room, walked downstairs, and had planned to walk out the door of the hospital and disappear for good. "I went back upstairs because I told you I'd be here and I didn't want to let you down. If it wasn't for you guys, I wouldn't be here now."

He called the next day and sang on my answering machine. And he laughed that laugh that made me laugh and then made me cry. "I used to sing with the Mississippi Mass Choir," he told me. Another slice of his life came out.

We continued to press him to call his family. He finally called his sister Cynthia. My sister, with her generous, lavish heart, offered to fly Cynthia to Denver *and* rent her a car. Cynthia had no idea he was so sick.

"I don't understand why he didn't call us sooner! I would have come before this."

He had distanced himself from his family for reasons they still don't understand. It was obvious they loved him. But life had hurt him deeply somehow.

Cynthia came out, and one night at his apartment she shared her heart. "You know, I've had some back problems and I haven't been able to work, but I've felt like there must be something I should be doing. 'Lord,' I prayed, 'what is my purpose? What do you want me to do?' Well, this is the answer. I'm supposed to take Tony home and take care of him."

The Veterans Administration paid for Tony's flight, and my sister paid for Cynthia's flight. When Tony went home, I knew I would never see him again.

His family flocked to see their lamb that had strayed. His brothers and sisters came from all over the country, and his daughters came — yes, he had two daughters and four grandchildren! His story kept unfolding.

His mom never left his side. She called me one day and told me, "I had been praying for a miracle for my Tony, and you were that miracle." Tony died that May. He fell asleep and never woke up, but he died with his family around him. He wasn't alone anymore.

Tony's family included our family photo in his funeral program with the following words: "We could not have had a better family than you to take care of our beloved Tony. Saying thank you is not enough! You deserve more. May God bless you and keep you."

I took a chance to tip my heart and let some lavish love spill out, and look what happened: a very unexpected love story.

— *Tamara Vermeer*

Sometimes in life we take a chance on someone. That decision makes the stomach tilt and our hands a little shaky. We don't have to do it, no one will know if we don't, and our lives would continue the same as always. But when we start to love, not only as a tentative experiment but also lavishly, our lives are changed forever. When we love generously, we receive unforgettable rewards. And sometimes, that caring touches not only the other person but has a ripple effect, creating an "extended family" that becomes an experience of true community that we all long for.

THE POTATO FIASCO

"Don, dear," I said, "will you keep a *wee* eye on the potatoes?"

"What am I supposed to do with them?" my husband asked.

Breathe deeply, Eileen, just be patient and talk sweetly, I reminded myself.

I was pleased I'd resisted the urge to ask him if he was stupid.

"Just watch them, and when they're cooked, take them off the stove and mash them," I replied with as much patience as I could muster.

Pretty simple, wouldn't you think?

We both work full-time. Over the years we've tried to negotiate household tasks fairly. When one cooks (mostly me) the other cleans up. Don does most of the shopping and I take care of tasks around the house. He's in charge of car maintenance and bills, and I organize the vacations. And so it goes; it works well for us.

On this day, of what's now known as the "potato fiasco," I'd prepared the meal. The potatoes were almost ready when I remembered I needed to get to the bank before closing time.

On my return to the neighborhood thirty minutes later, the smell of smoke tickled my sensitive nostrils as I turned onto our street.

There's a house on fire, I thought.

When I reached our driveway, my nose and my stomach rebelled. The windows and doors were wide open, and as I walked into the house I shivered with cold. Bits of potatoes were splattered all over the stove, the countertops, and the floor.

"What on earth happened here?" I screeched.

My limited patience and understanding flew out the gaping patio door, where my eyes spotted the blackened pot cowering under the freshly melted rungs of the garden chair.

"How did the chair get burned?" I interrogated.

"Well, I put the pot on it," Don replied.

"On plastic? On *plastic?*" I squawked parrot-fashion. "How could you be so stupid?"

There they were — the words. I accused my husband of being stupid. That signaled a *biggie* was about to blow.

The phrases swirled around the kitchen and outdid the smoke.

"How on earth could you? I can never trust you to do anything simple."

In relationships, it's very easy for me to let seemingly small things blow out of proportion. For me, this incident was about a lack of listening and caring. For Don, it was no big deal; we could just buy another pot (and another lawn chair!).

The unfettered words and phrases spewed out and took on a life of their own. I *knew* I needed to take a time-out and breathe deeply, but the foul air in the kitchen moved me to the verge of throwing up. I *knew* losing my temper and acting like a toddler wasn't a solution, but knowledge deserted me and joined the burnt pot on the patio. I exploded like the potatoes. Between fumes, I told myself I couldn't stay in a house with such a disgusting smell.

I went on an internal roll.

I'm fed up with a husband who just won't listen to me and leaves me to do everything.

Why couldn't he follow simple instructions and complete a simple task?

Surely watching a pot of potatoes boil isn't rocket science?

The more I internalized, the angrier I

became. Then my martyr mode arrived in full glory in the universal mantle of *never* and *always.*

Just because I'm a woman I always *end up doing all the cooking.*

If I didn't cook, we'd never *eat at home and we'd be even poorer.*

If it wasn't for my cooking, we'd go hungry most of the time; he never *cooks.*

When the negative spirals hit, I lose all common sense. I'm sure a more mature and spiritually enlightened person might ask: "Were you having severe PMS or menopausal symptoms?" "Were you in your very early twenties when this incident happened?" "Were you on serious medication with severe side effects?"

I have to confess the answer to all these questions is *no.*

I'm old enough to know better. Common sense isn't always so common in my life.

I stormed from the house and slammed the door. I drove to the nearby lake, parked the car, put my head on the steering wheel, and screeched — one of those howlers that frightened the birds, stirred the waters, and shook the lake. Then I had one glorious cry. At times, marriage seems to be the hardest relationship in the world.

I wailed the prayer of the blind man in

the Gospels. When Jesus asked him what he wanted, the man's reply was simple: "Lord . . . I want to see!" (Luke 18:41).

I repeated this verse over and over and added:

"Lord, just let me see what I need to do and how I need to be."

I rarely get instant answers to my prayer (or perhaps I do, but I'm often slow on the uptake).

I drove back to the house and stormed into the kitchen. I looked at the stove and then at my husband, who made the mistake of saying, "You overreacted."

The blaming words sizzled unspoken between us again, but this time I remembered our time-out rule. I went to the bedroom, closed the door, and flung my injured ego on the bed. For my highly intelligent husband, it was still only about a stupid pot. For me, it was about his not listening to me, not doing things for me, and taking me for granted.

It was about — about — about — control! *Yuck!*

Don't you just hate those moments when God gives you the insight you asked for?

My husband found his common sense quicker than I did. He tapped on the bedroom door.

"Would you like a *wee* cup of tea?" he asked.

It was my native Irish *wee,* said with an American accent, that did it, as well as the fact that he'd offered *to do something for me.*

Don ventured in with the cup of tea and placed it on the bedside table. He accompanied his gracious offering with a verbal gift: "I'm sorry, dear. I didn't listen. You don't often ask me to do much. I'm sorry. Will you forgive me?"

After a somewhat sulky silence, I looked at the *wee* cup of tea and then at Don. I followed his lead.

"I'm sorry too."

Eat your heart out, Ryan O'Neal and Ali MacGraw. In their classic movie *Love Story* the big theme was "Love means never having to say you're sorry." If you love someone you automatically forgive anything they do that is wrong.

But part of my love story involves saying, "I'm sorry."

What would we do without those little words? They're especially important to my husband. He communicates his love to others and to me by his words, while I prefer to show my love through doing things for him.

Don often reminded me it's important to attack our problems and not each other. Of course, I *knew* all that. I also knew we'd developed some simple communication rules in our relationship, like using "I" statements and taking a time-out when things got heated.

I knew I'd messed up badly and behaved like a spoiled brat. Those seemingly simple words — *I'm sorry* — combined with the cup of tea cleared the air for both of us. Once I'd uttered them, and taken a few sips of my Irish nectar, I moved into a more rational space. We talked. We listened to each other's feelings. Once we agreed we'd both been heard and understood, we prayed together.

The mood shifted. We shared hugs and dinner — without potatoes.

— *Eileen Roddy*

As Eileen alluded to, one of the popular sayings of the 1970s was "Love means never having to say you're sorry." When we've lost control of our tongues, we like to pretend this maxim is true. We like to think, "Well, she knows I didn't mean it." Admitting culpability is so hard to do!

But when our tempers flare and our words wound, the first step to healing is a simple

34

apology.

Some wise words from the most practical book ever written, the Bible, point out that if we could control our tongues, we would be perfect and could also control ourselves in every other way (see James 3:2).

Unfortunately, most of us fall way short of perfection, saying many things we know we shouldn't — and most often to those we love the most. When we hurt others with our tongues, we can also start the healing process with a simple verbal apology.

THE CHANGELING

I never thought I would have to learn to love my son, Jonathan, twice. The first time I fell hopelessly in love with him took place during the nine months he resided in my womb. The moment he came screaming into this world, red and wrinkled with a head full of black hair, he captured my heart as completely as his sister had seven years earlier.

By the time Jonathan turned four, a mischievous smile played across his face most of the time. He loved to hide a small artificial flower arrangement behind his back and try to surprise me. "I brought you flowers, Mommy," he would say to me, clutching the flowers in his hand and looking very pleased with himself.

Even when he misbehaved and my husband or I had to discipline him, he never remained upset for long. Happiness surrounded him and he brought joy into our lives.

When Jonathan was five years old, weight loss, hemorrhaging, and severe abdominal pain hounded him. We feared that he had cancer, but the diagnosis came back ulcerative colitis. His doctor cautioned us that he'd never seen such a severe case in a child of Jonathan's age, but we focused on thanking God that he didn't have cancer. Though we knew nothing about colitis, we assumed medication could restore him to health.

However, our lives soon lost all sense of normalcy. Jonathan spent more time hospitalized than at home, and continued to grow worse. Either my husband or I stayed with him twenty-four hours a day, while also trying to squeeze in time with his sister.

Three days before his seventh birthday, Jonathan experienced a grand mal seizure and lapsed into a coma. We grieved and tried to prepare for the inevitable. One week crept by, then two with no change. Our hopes rose when he began to slowly emerge from the coma.

We soon learned that though he could move his limbs and react to pain, something was terribly wrong. A CAT scan revealed he had suffered a stroke, causing permanent brain damage.

I refused to accept the fact that he would never recover. We sang to him and propped all his favorite toys in front of him, attempting to stimulate his mind. We sought treatment through neurologists, speech pathologists, psychologists, and prayer. We begged God to restore our son. Jonathan's speech gradually returned, albeit on a two- or three-year-old level, and his health improved.

But Jonathan had changed. Our happy, playful seven-year-old had been transformed into a hyperactive, angry two-year-old that we didn't recognize.

"I hate you" and "You're dumb and stupid" spewed from his mouth frequently. He never smiled and only said negative words. We grieved over our loss as though he had died. In fact, the child that we had previously known had indeed died.

How could I learn to love this hostile stranger in my house? I determined to demonstrate love to him every time he was unlovable. When he screamed his verbal venom, I wrapped my arms around him and refused to let go until he calmed down. We sought the help of a behavioral psychologist and committed to follow her recommendations no matter how difficult.

Gradually, we saw improvements. By the

time he turned eight, Jonathan had recovered enough to return to school, and after extensive testing, a committee decided he would benefit from a special education center. Even though I struggled, fluctuating between acceptance and denial of his mental state, I finally agreed to the transfer. It proved to be the best decision we could have made.

Shirley, Jonathan's new teacher, was determined to help him relearn as much as his mental capacity would allow. She drilled him relentlessly on the alphabet, numbers, and colors, and used every situation as a learning opportunity.

But more important than that, she loved him and accepted him — exactly as he was. And I was learning to love him again as well.

We enrolled Jonathan in Special Olympics. He had demonstrated an inclination toward running away, so we got him into a track competition. The day of the race dawned sunny and warm. Excitement filled the air. When his turn came, Jonathan ran freely, leaving the other athletes behind. He won the first of many gold medals that day.

Jonathan's behavior continued to improve over the years. However, the most beautiful transformation took place in his heart. I realized what a drastic change it was one day when we pulled into a fast-food drive-through to buy a soda.

In the past Jonathan had always yelled out the window, "You're dumb and stupid and I hate you!"

But now he screamed, "You're pretty and nice and I love you!"

Both statements always took the teenage employee off guard, but at least the new one brought a smile!

By the time Jonathan reached middle-school age, his teachers recommended he be transferred to a special education class in a regular school setting. The special education center had been wonderful for him, but we knew it was time for him to return to his neighborhood school. I was awake many nights with fears about how Jonathan's former peers would receive him. My concerns proved to be unfounded. Everyone accepted Jonathan and welcomed him back. Though labeled "severely mentally disabled," Jonathan continued to improve.

High school provided another challenge. How would he survive with so many students rushing through the halls? What if he got lost? What if students made fun of disabled kids?

Once again my fears were for nothing.

Every day "peer helpers" took Jonathan with them to the cafeteria, helped him purchase his lunch, and sat with him during the meal. One of the football players played catch with him outside on sunny days. They even selected him for "student of the month" and posted his name in the cafeteria!

We approached high school graduation with mixed feelings. We were thankful for the progress Jonathan had made over the years, but apprehensive over his future. The week before the ceremony, we received a letter inviting us to attend an award ceremony. We thought it was a mistake. We were astonished to discover that they had given him an award for all his accomplishments with Special Olympics over the years.

My heart swelled with pride the morning of his graduation. He looked so handsome in his cap and gown as he sat with all the other graduates. When they called his name, his teacher accompanied him up the steps and across the stage. Suddenly the entire senior class stood and burst into applause! A standing ovation for our special guy!

I realized in that moment, with tears streaming down my face, that I had never stopped loving him. He had changed tremendously when he suffered the stroke, but I had changed as well. I had learned not only to accept him exactly as he was but also to open my heart to accept all people with disabilities and to look beyond their limitations.

Jonathan will always be my special child no matter what hand life deals us. And I will love him forever, exactly as he is.

— *Louise D. Flanders*

Life happens. The unexpected can occur in any of our lives at any time. Most of us are very cognizant of that fact — so much so that we may easily fall into the trap of worrying about all the "what ifs" that we someday might have to face.

The more seasoned fretters and planners among us even think of the potential effect tragedies might have on our relationships. "How will I cope with my husband if he becomes an invalid?" "How can I keep on loving my child if he keeps making bad choices and spiraling in the downward direction he's going?" "How will I feel about my children if they ever face an illness that leaves them mentally incapacitated and unpleasant?" "What if I have to deal with embarrassment or frustration or humiliation because of their behavior?"

Thankfully, Louise reminds us that although life happens and tragedies ensue, love has the ability to adapt. Somehow love is flexible and strong enough to step up to the challenges it faces. When we encounter distressing situations, love has a deep reservoir we may not see but we can still draw from.

A SIMPLE CUP OF CHEER

I carefully parted the curtains and peeked out the window of the warm, dark motel room; I wanted our three young children to sleep just a little longer. White feathers of snow were drifting down to blanket the cars outside as the winter sun began to light the cold, blustery scene.

We had arrived in Carlsbad, New Mexico, the evening before with plans to take the children on a hike into McKittrick Canyon to see the fall foliage. This early snowstorm would cancel our hike, but we could still visit Carlsbad Caverns. A sign on the highway told us the cave was "56 degrees year-round."

My wife and I bundled the kids, all under ten, into their warm coats and blue jeans. All three were giggling about the snow and anticipating the day's adventures. After breakfast, we got them snuggled into the car under a warm blanket. We sang and

44

laughed as we drove through the winter landscape toward the caverns.

The snow blew across the main highway without much accumulation. However, when we turned off the main road, the snow was deeper. A National Park Service car stood in front of the gate to the seven-mile road into the park. Three rangers were sloshing through the freezing mush. As each of them stopped at the cars ahead of me, I noticed that some of the frustrated travelers seemed to be arguing with them.

When it was our turn, the young man who approached my window was wearing a park service uniform and a standard-issue jacket that looked better suited to the 56 degrees in the caverns than the current 26 degrees outside. Like the other rangers, he was in his early twenties. He looked tired, cold, and more than a little frustrated. I speculated that he was more comfortable with his usual job of answering interesting questions about the park than with today's job of delivering bad news.

"Good morning, sir. I am sorry; the conditions on the winding road into the park are not safe because of the snow. The Park Service has closed the park at least until tomorrow. You can call the Park number for updated information."

"Thanks for telling us. I know it's cold out there. We appreciate your looking out for us."

He looked relieved. "Thank you, sir. You have a nice day."

We turned the car around to head back to the motel. On the way, I noticed a coffee shop.

"How about some hot chocolate?"

"Hooray, Daddy! That sounds great!"

As we walked into the restaurant, the aroma of hot chocolate and coffee embraced us. The tables were crowded with families dressed in winter coats, hats, and scarves. As we sat down, we remembered our motel had a heated indoor pool and decided it would be fun to swim while there was snow on the ground.

I looked back out onto the cold, snowy terrain and realized being together as a family, splashing in a warm indoor pool, would be a lot more pleasant than what those rangers would be up against all day. Then I had an idea.

"Honey, why don't we get those rangers some hot coffee?"

"That's a great idea!"

I ordered three coffees to go and loaded up a cardboard tray with plenty of creamers and sugars. We got back into the car and headed to the entrance of the park. I pulled around the line of cars and stopped near the gate. Coffee in hand, I approached the nearest ranger.

"Hey, you guys look pretty cold out here. We thought you could use some hot coffee."

Obviously taken aback, he stammered, "Well, thank you. Thank you very much."

We watched him through the window of our car as he gave the coffee to his fellow rangers and gestured toward us. Seeing their happy faces was more fun than any hike.

As we drove back to the motel, we talked with the children about how cold those rangers must have been standing outside. We said our gift would give them warmth and encouragement that could last all day, because despite their important jobs, many people did not appreciate the work they did, and even made their jobs more difficult.

Later that day, I thought about the concept of random acts of kindness. Why is it such a rich tradition? Why is it so gratifying when we do it? Why is it so surprising to those it benefits?

If I'm honest, I'll admit that sometimes I have been just as frustrated, and perhaps *almost* as unpleasant, as the travelers who argued with the rangers. We *all* go through life preoccupied with our own plans. We tend to view other people who disrupt us as *adversaries* rather than as those who are simply trying to do their job. No wonder we treat them badly and ignore their feelings.

Why did I take the high road *this* time?

I was in a different mind-set that snowy November day. I was focusing on my wife and children. I wanted *them* to have a good time. I was grateful for our time together, even though the weather had already changed our plans once. I was on vacation and didn't have much of an agenda. Perhaps because I was looking outward, I noticed the humanness of those rangers. I empathized with their problems and their suffering. *I saw them as people just like me.*

So many times I see people only in their roles as park ranger, salesclerk, bank teller, or whatever. I forget that they are mothers, daughters, brothers, friends. The lesson I learned that day was that when I interact with people, I need to look beyond their job descriptions and see them as fellow human beings, even friends. I have to realize that they have their own desires, plans, hurts, and stresses. I want to reach out and be an encourager. If I do a better job of loving strangers, they may be more loving to me and to others, and all our lives will be richer for it.

The next evening as we rode home together, we watched the sun set over the melting snow. Reflecting on our weekend, we decided our small gesture of serving coffee to the rangers warmed us as much as it did them.

— *Steven L. Brown*

"Each one, reach one."

"Reach out and touch someone."

"Let it begin with me."

Over the years, dozens of marketing slogans and even more songs have encouraged us to express kindness, understanding, and even love to others.

Our actions don't have to be grand gestures or extraordinary behaviors to make a difference in someone's day. They can be small things, such as a smile, a friendly word, or even a cup of coffee.

When we get in the habit and express these light touches of caring, not only do we make the world a better place but we also make our own lives better. We become more loving people, and fostering such an attitude offers its own wonderful reward.

DRINKING MILK
WITH A SPOON

"I've never been to a more beautiful service," my friend Kathy said after the memorial for my husband. "How did you and Duane manage to have such a loving and close family?"

I was hearing this comment over and over. It was true. We were blessed with forty-seven years together, three children in strong marriages, and eight grandchildren. They all produced an extraordinary tribute to a man they dearly loved.

What no one knew was how close our relationship came to ending in shambles one blustery winter evening. That night I realized my love for my husband no longer existed.

Clink! Clink! Clink! I looked up from my knitting at the source of the annoying sound. My husband of eleven years sat in front of the television, drinking his chocolate milk with a *spoon*. I felt a familiar disgust at this habit.

Duane had a practical reason for downing his drink this way. Overweight, he could easily gulp two or three glasses. Using a spoon, he only drank one.

But more than the constant clinking bothered me. Duane was difficult to live with. When not criticizing me, he often sat silent, reluctant to communicate for long periods of time.

He'd changed so much since the Thanksgiving weekend we'd first met. An eighteen-year-old freshman at the University of Portland, I planned to become a teacher and was the least likely of my friends to marry young. At twenty-two, Duane already held a good job and was looking to settle down.

Our chance meeting quickly developed into a romance. School and career no longer mattered. He asked me to marry him on our second date, and I agreed on our third. I quit school, and we married the following April.

The marriage shouldn't have had a chance. We were too young and impetuous.

Our first years together were happy, and three babies promptly joined us. I couldn't remember when things changed, but as I looked at the father of my children that night, the heat from the blazing logs in the fireplace did nothing to warm my cold heart.

Divorce was not an option. No one in either of our families had taken that route. We were both committed to the institution of marriage, even if it had become a prison.

I got up from my chair and walked into the kitchen. *Oh, Lord* — the words silently tore from my heart — *how can I live another fifty years with this man? There must be a way to make our life better.*

Reacting to a sudden urge, I got out paper and pencil, sat down at the kitchen table, and wrote a list of my husband's faults. When finished, I stared for several minutes at the five things written on the sheet. Two of them were truly unattractive traits, one being his constant criticism. I kept trying to add to the list, but couldn't. I felt the deepest disgust at his drinking his chocolate milk with a spoon.

I don't understand, I thought. *Why do I feel so hostile over these few things?*

On another sheet of paper I recorded Duane's good qualities. This list was long and included many characteristics that first attracted me to him: a great sense of humor; a strong work ethic that made him a good provider; he put family before anything else; he was a terrific father; and he coached the children in sports. The list went on and on.

This is a wonderful man, I thought. *Why do I feel such animosity toward him?*

Comprehension slowly broke through my bewilderment. My focus had been on Duane's few imperfections to the point that I no longer saw any of his positive traits.

Another sheet of paper came out, and one by one I wrote out *my* good qualities. My list of good points was only slightly longer than Duane's list of faults.

Then I tackled my own negative list. I wrote, and wrote, and wrote. And then wrote some more. My pencil traced down the page, revealing many of my flaws. I examined them closely and realized that changes in these areas would make me a better person.

I stared at the four lists before me. After going back and forth from page to page, I could not escape the truth.

Why does this man stay married to me? I wondered.

Looking at things in black and white often brings clarity. We both were caught up in a circle of negativity, each reacting to the other. I saw Duane's suggestions as criticism and responded by turning on him. He retaliated in such a way that his suggestions turned to criticisms, which made me even more angry.

I took the list of Duane's faults into the front room and, right in front of him, threw it onto the burning embers in the fireplace. It was a symbolic action. As I watched the paper brown and curl, the last remnants disappearing in ashes and smoke, I put to death all thoughts of the things I'd written on it.

Duane was oblivious to what I was doing. He was still drinking his chocolate milk with a spoon.

Back in the kitchen, I charted a course of action, and then began to follow it.

First, I read the list of Duane's good qualities several times and put them in my purse. During the next week, I read them over ten times a day, then once a day the next week. For the next month, I read them once a week. I kept that list for years, finding and rereading it whenever I bought a new purse.

Second, I focused on my own lists. Looking at my good qualities, I realized that I had a foundation on which to build. I went to work changing my behavior on each of the negative traits.

I didn't tell Duane of my eye-opening experience. I think I was afraid that if he saw how justified his criticism was he might leave me. I also felt that it was more important for him to see actual change in me than to hear words.

Surprisingly, I soon gained new respect for my husband and my love returned richer than ever. As I changed for the better, Duane treated me with renewed love and respect and his criticism ceased. I will never understand why, but a week after that night, he stopped drinking his chocolate milk with a spoon!

This happened thirty-six years ago. After that we came to enjoy the deep love that comes when two people grow together for many years.

When I think back to that night so long ago, I know my commitment to marriage gave me the desire to improve my relationship with Duane. But God heard my frustrated cry, gave me the idea to take up paper and pencil, and helped me regain my lost love for my husband.

— *Doris E. Clark*

The most valuable book ever written, the Bible, tells us, "Fix your thoughts on what is true, and honorable, and right, and pure, and lovely, and admirable. Think about things that are excellent and worthy of praise" (Philippians 4:8).

What valuable advice for all of us in all areas

of life — but especially in relationships! The old saying "Familiarity breeds contempt" tends to be true. Whenever we live with or spend many hours with someone else, before long we start seeing the faults in that person's life. If we let them, little faults tend to become magnified and may soon be the crack in the mortar of our relationships.

As Doris discovered, one way to overcome the contempt of familiarity is to put the faults in perspective — to compare the severity of the negative elements in a loved one's life with the positive attributes that person displays.

And then the trick is to close our eyes to irritating factors — consciously ignore, or even burn the list — and only focus on the positive.

As we consciously look only at the good things, before long that's all we see.

The Hug I'll Never Forget

You need to spend the night with Daddy, I scolded myself as I drove down the highway. *You always stay with your parents when you go to visit them, not at your sister's house.*

My dad was a silent, impenetrable fortress, hiding behind a stern stare or a curt comment. For most of my thirty-five years I either ignored him or attempted, without success, to have him acknowledge me or my accomplishments.

Neither extreme satisfied me. When I steered clear of him, I avoided face-to-face rejection, but I still longed to have a relationship with him. Often when I engaged him in conversation, his gruff responses hurt my feelings. I felt trapped in a no-win situation.

My relationship with my mother was much different. Even though my parents and I lived a hundred and twenty-five miles apart, Mother and I shared our feelings in weekly letters and telephone calls. Mother knew I longed for a better relationship with Daddy but had no suggestions on how to obtain it. Her understanding and hugs helped but did not eliminate my desire to feel close to Daddy.

Throughout this struggle, I harbored a dark secret, one I did not even share with Mother. I was afraid that even though Daddy was older than Mother, she would die first, leaving me to cope with my uncommunicative father. My fear became reality when Mother was diagnosed with bone cancer. The prognosis: three to four years.

While coping with Mother's debilitating disease, I pondered how I would manage staying alone in the house with my father during visits since Mother had been moved to a skilled care facility.

So on the two-hour drive to visit my mother, I argued with myself: *You need to spend the night with Daddy.*

Yeah, but I'll be miserable; he won't even say six words to me.

A good daughter would visit her father.

Maybe so, but he's not a very good father; he rarely speaks to me.

I thought of the college education Daddy had given my sisters and me, not asking us to contribute a dime.

Yeah, but Daddy never once asked what I planned to do with my education or what grades I got.

I had never lacked food or clothing.

Yeah, but I had to wear hand-me-downs from my older sisters. I never wore the latest styles. Daddy was too frugal to let me dress like other girls.

I thought of the cost of our family's summer vacations, introducing us to a number of states, parts of Canada, and a wealth of scenery and museums.

Yeah, but we always stayed in some out-of-the-way place. Not on the beach or in the mountains.

Every positive thought I had about my father was negated by unhappy memories. While I bemoaned my fate, several Bible verses sprang to mind, among them: *"We love because he first loved us"* (1 John 4:19 NIV) and *"While we were still sinners, Christ died for us"* (Romans 5:8 NIV).

The depth of God's love overwhelmed me. He loved us when we were not worthy of being loved.

Suddenly I thought of a slogan I'd often used when counseling alcoholics: "Fake it 'til you make it."

This clarified what I must do. I would treat my father as if he had been the perfect loving father I had always dreamed of having. No matter what his response, I would let him know I cared for him. I would not wait for his love; I would give mine first.

That night Daddy and I ate the supper he'd prepared. I complimented him on the meal. No response.

After supper I cleaned up the kitchen and then joined him in the living room. We sat across the room from each other reading our sections of the paper in silence. At ten, he announced he was going to bed, leaving me to turn off the lights.

The next morning, I planned to visit Mother at the care facility and then drive home. Daddy walked me outside. Before getting into my car, I put my arms around him. "Bye, Daddy. I love you."

I didn't get any splinters in my body, but hugging him was like grasping a wooden pole; his arms never moved from his sides.

Several weeks later on Father's Day, I had no desire to call my father, but told myself, "Act as if you have the best father in the world."

I wished Daddy a happy Father's Day and asked about his garden, a topic that always generated a few comments. He told me about pulling radishes and taking some to Mother at the care center, shooing rabbits away from the sprouting green beans, and preparing to cut asparagus.

"I love you, Daddy," I said at the end of the conversation.

Daddy said, "Bye."

Later that week I called Mother. "Your father told me he was happy that you called him on Father's Day," she said.

Why can't he tell me *that?* I wondered.

For the next nine months, while Mother's cancer ate away at her bones, I continued my one-sided expression of love to Daddy. In March, I joined him to celebrate our birthdays, which are ten days apart. I looked at his array of birthday cards on the mantel.

"You got a card from Francine?" My older sister had forgotten my birthday. "She didn't remember my birthday at all."

Daddy responded, "What's a card? Nothing but a piece of paper."

"I know, Daddy, but . . ."

"I just said that so you wouldn't feel so bad."

Hearing Daddy explain stunned me. I had always thought Daddy had no feelings since he never expressed any, but under his stony façade he had emotions and was concerned about mine. Now I was the speechless one.

Months later on another visit, I told Daddy, "You know, I really appreciate your

61

paying for my college education. Thank you, Daddy."

He turned away from me. "I never thought I'd live long enough to hear anyone thank me."

All my life I wanted his love and recognition, and now I realized he craved the same thing.

He left the room, and I thought about the number of times he'd done special things for me: buying chocolate-dipped ice cream cones at the Dairy Queen, a special treat that only we shared; giving me a Pogo Stick one Christmas, a gift I couldn't master so he demonstrated how it worked, which brought laughter to both of us; attending my school plays and concerts; sharing his love of gardening; setting up his telescope to show me the craters on the moon; making a bug cage for me to catch fireflies. How often had I thanked him? Not nearly enough.

Having studied psychology in college, I knew the importance of feeling accepted. How sad that at eighty years old my father — who was a college graduate, a successful chemical engineer, and one of the smartest people I knew — couldn't freely give or receive love.

My plan to treat Daddy as if he was the

best father in the world succeeded, despite my selfish motive. Daddy really *was* the best father in the world. He had given me all that he had to give: his love of gardening, an inquisitive mind, and the education and skills to be self-sufficient.

Six months later Mother died. I continued my weekly telephone calls to Daddy and visited him several times a year for the next four years. Each time I visited, I hugged him good-bye and told him I loved him, and as usual Daddy stood rigid, saying nothing.

The last time I visited him, shortly before he died of a heart attack, when I hugged him his right arm moved from his side and he patted my back. Then he quickly put his arm back at his side. That little pat happened fifteen years ago, but I can still recall the sensation of the best Daddy in the world giving me a hug.

— *Rebecca Willman Gernon*

Human nature often impels us to look at others in our lives and cry, "But you don't care. I can only love you if you love me." Our human nature tends to withhold and wait to give until we're sure we'll get benefits for our emotional time and trouble.

But how contrary human nature Is to true love! When we long for someone to change, sometimes the best step to take is the first step — acting not on the way things are but on the way we wish a relationship to be. Choosing to have faith in a relationship is always a risk. But more often than not, when we're willing to take the first step, changes happen — in us and in those we long to be close to.

Between Mountain Streams and Ferris Wheels

As the sun rose in the sky, I tried to read, but lost my place several times and kept reading the same sentence over and over. Instead of concentrating on the words, my head throbbed with thoughts of *How dare he!*

Just a few steps from the car, my husband stood casting his fishing line toward the lake, perfectly at peace.

A fine mist fell from the sky as birds, ducks, frogs, and crickets sang a marvelous melody, a perfect blending of their "voices." Even the occasional splashing of the fish fit the harmony.

Marvin looked the picture of serenity standing on the edge of the lake, fishing pole extended. While I sulked in the car, he had the audacity to enjoy himself, not noticing how miserable I was.

This was early in our marriage, and becoming one was proving to be more of a fairy tale than a reality. We were at Split Rock in the Pocono Mountains, one of the most stunning and romantic locations I had ever seen.

The setting made me envision every love story I'd ever read, and every romantic movie I'd ever seen came alive, with my husband and me as the main characters. I envisioned us holding hands, taking long walks, cuddling, and just shutting out the world. I wanted to experience the passion and the closeness of a couple so deeply in love they could exchange skin and still not be close enough.

Unfortunately, that was not the same idea my husband had in mind for the trip. On that anniversary, I hadn't yet learned the freedom of individual as well as shared activities.

Through the years, I started to learn about compromise, the mutual give-and-take that makes relationships work. One of the most pertinent lessons came the first time Marvin and I took our kids to Ocean City, Maryland, a renowned beach town.

I loved to get up at daybreak and walk the beach. I reveled in every sound, from the waves crashing to the seagulls squealing. I watched the beach come alive with the rising sun. The dolphins swam in their own little pack as if they were accompanying me on my walk. In the distance, a huge ocean liner inched by on what looked like the edge of the earth.

I wasn't alone in the morning journey; other early birds arrived to begin fishing while young couples cuddled together as the sun climbed.

Later in the day I followed the kids as they raced toward the ocean. I stepped quickly as the hot sand burned my feet.

"Come on, Mom!" the kids yelled as they splashed in the water.

"Is it cold?" I screamed back.

"No, Mom, the water is great. Come on in."

As I stepped into the frigid water, I held my breath. The deeper I went the more the waves tried to pull me out, the coldness sending shock waves through me. After a few moments of mommy time, I sat on the beach, enjoying the salty air while the sun baked me or my children buried me in the sand.

After a long day of soaking in the sun, we showered, changed, and went to the board-walk, along with thousands of other vaca-tioners. The warm air blended with the sweet smell of caramel popcorn and cotton candy along the twenty-seven-block stretch.

Laughter, talking, and music filled the air. The dark night sky was illuminated with carnival-ride lights. The warm, cozy feeling of walking hand in hand with the love of my life made me want to get even closer to him.

I turned, expecting the same expression of delight on Marvin's face. Instead, I saw that he was frowning, his eyebrows furrowed down under his baseball cap.

"What's wrong?" I asked.

"Nothing," he answered.

The kids were hopping on cloud nine as they enjoyed the best of a child's world: burgers, boardwalk fries, funnel cakes, rides, games, and prizes. Shawn and Shannon made as much noise as they wanted. However, my husband was quietly suffering, all for the sake of compromise and his family's happiness.

I knew Marvin would rather sleep in or fish on his vacation than walk the shoreline before the crack of dawn. I knew he didn't like the heat, so sometimes he didn't join us on the beach. However, I didn't know just how much Marvin really hated the beach in general.

I learned on that trip that he loathed the feeling of sand on his skin. Within ten minutes of even a particle of sand touching his body, he craved a shower. As for the boardwalk, sharing a small space with hundreds of strangers didn't exactly enhance his life either.

He enjoys freshwater fishing for long hours, and I enjoy walking long distances. I could take a little fishing and he could take a little walking, but neither of us could take the less likeable activity for an extended time period. A long walk to him is equivalent to walking to the mailbox, so the twenty-seven blocks of walking shoulder to shoulder with other vacationers must have been to him like a marathon fishing trip would be to me — murder.

I was amazed at this revelation, because although he didn't look comfortable at the beach, he certainly didn't display the misery that I had displayed at the mountains a few years earlier.

Watching Marvin on that trip, I learned that love might mean sacrificing your preferences for the sake of others. Give-and-take is not so bad if both parties contribute.

In the spirit of compromise, I even learned to like a part of Marvin's world that I probably would otherwise never have tried. I get a fishing license each year and enjoy the fishing trips we make to local ponds and lakes. I often watch the hunting and fishing shows on television with Marvin. I even passed the hunting safety course so I could go hunting with him.

Last season, he took me on a turkey hunt. The first thing I learned was that getting up at three AM is hard, even for an early bird like me. But once I had on my camouflage gear and was walking in the woods behind my husband, I found it exciting and relaxing.

We stepped slowly and quietly to a place my husband had scouted earlier, and he managed to locate it even in the dark. As the world around us was rousing, we sat still on two tiny triangular seats in a make-shift tent. My husband grabbed a little wooden box and a stick and scratched several times, paused, and repeated.

The high-pitched sounds pierced my ears and echoed through the woods. Then a faint sound came back. Marvin's back straightened, his lips adjusted, and he made a loud squawk with the turkey caller in his mouth. Silence, then a similar sound returned. Marvin answered the call with the same tone and beat.

The squawk was getting closer with each exchange of communication between Marvin and the turkey. I was on the edge of my seat, holding my breath, and feeling like an unknown language was being spoken.

I looked at my husband, and his eyes shone with the same pleasure that I displayed at the beach. We were in his element, and he enjoyed my company just as I enjoyed his at the beach.

Most people who know me could not believe that I, afraid of spiders, sat in the woods on a hunt. But that is the power of compromise inspired by love: When we give and take, the unbelievable becomes possible and even enjoyable.

— *Sheila Farmer*

In our idealistic relationship fantasies, we sometimes assume or expect that others have the same goals and enjoyments that we do. How shocking, then, to learn that something that thrills our hearts — like walking on the beach — is torture to the person we care about!

When we learn about these differences, we face choices. Some people in a relationship just pursue their own interests, giving each other freedom to go separate ways. Some of this can be good. But on the other hand, it can lead to each person just doing his or her own thing — and that can end up causing problems in a marriage.

As Sheila and Marvin found, compromise can make all the difference. At times they each sacrifice their preferences, to some degree, to please the other. They try to keep abreast of each other's interests and partici- pate enough to understand the joy the other person derives from the activity. The focus is not on doing something they hate, but on giv- ing in a little here and there, being flexible and understanding, and showing a willingness to support the other.

Compromise in a relationship is not only a good goal but necessary for the relationship to grow and fully develop.

THE LITTLE GIRL WHO CHANGED MY LIFE

When new neighbors moved in next door, I didn't pay much attention since trees and brush made a barrier between our country properties. But before long I was made very aware of the children . . . one in particular.

My husband and I don't have children, and for years our lives only included the two of us. When I retired early from my job at the public library, I pretty much did what I wanted, when I wanted.

One afternoon as I weeded the kitchen garden, I heard a voice behind me.

"Will you play with me?"

I turned around and saw a cute little girl about four years old. She wore a flowered dress and her feet were bare. Part of her brown hair was pulled away from her face with a rubber band. When she moved, the rest fell around her chipmunk-like cheeks.

"I'm busy."

"I'm Libby."

"I'm Mrs. Perkins."

"Will you play with me?"

"How did you get over here?"

"I came through there."

She pointed at an opening under the trees and around my lilacs that made a perfect path from her front yard to our backyard.

"Does your mother know you're here?"

"She said, 'Go outside and play.' Will you play with me?"

I was annoyed. I had so much to do!

"What do you want to play?"

"House!"

I pulled off my gloves and followed her as she walked under the pine trees that divided our properties. She chattered about where the living room and kitchen would be. She wanted to be the mother and I was to be her little girl.

"I have to get back to work," I finally told her, pushing my way out from under the tree. I was hot and sweaty, with pine needles in my hair. "I think it's time for you to go home, too."

I thought that would be the end of it. I was wrong. That was the beginning of daily unannounced visits at all times.

I was cooking and heard a small fist pounding on the kitchen door. With a deep sigh I turned around.

"What are you doing?"

"Cooking."

"Can I help?"

"No."

"Please. Can I stir something?"

"Why don't you help your mom cook at home?"

"She's working."

"Who's taking care of you?"

"The baby-sitter."

"Okay." I shook my head in annoyance. "Stir this." I handed her something she couldn't spill.

Each day, if I heard a noise, I would tense . . . listening. Would I be able to continue what I was working on or would I be interrupted? Each time I went outside to work in the yard or garden, I peeked out the window first to be sure she wasn't around and then hurried into the garden to work, hiding so she wouldn't find me.

When I'd hear her saying, "What are you doing?" my heart would sink, as I knew I'd have to stop what I was doing. Then I'd feel guilty and ask God to forgive my bad attitude. I kept telling myself, "This little girl is more important than my tasks. Why am I so selfish with my time?"

Then one day she discovered I liked telling stories.

"What are you doing?"

"Reading."

"Will you read to me?"

"You wouldn't like my book."

"Will you tell me a story?"

I put down my book.

"What kind of story?"

"A story about me," she hesitated, then added, "and you."

"Once there was a little girl who had a friend. They would travel around the world with their animal companions, Monkey and Eagle."

A little more of my heart opened to her as she listened avidly.

The story of Libby, Mrs. Perkins, and their animal friends was never-ending — with new adventures inside caves, on islands, and near volcanoes all over the world. We'd sit on my swing and I would ask, "Now, where did we leave off?"

She always knew where that was. I especially loved these times together.

When Libby started going to school, her visits moved to afternoons. My husband put a wireless doorbell next to the kitchen door for her to use. One day I showed her how to change the kind of rings it would make. I never knew what to expect, especially since one of the tones was also that of the front door. She and I finally decided that Big Ben's bong would be her own special musical sound.

One afternoon Libby's sister Katie ran through the trees to see if I'd seen Libby.

"No. Why?"

"She got angry and ran away. Can you help me find her?"

"Is your mom at home?"

"No. I'm supposed to watch Libby and we had a fight."

"Which way did she go?"

Libby had run through several neighbors' backyards in her bare feet. I followed Katie through the yards and we began our search.

"There she is!" Katie pointed to a small figure between two houses.

"Libby!" I yelled. She ran away from us.

I called again and ran after her. When I finally caught up with her, she was crying.

"Libby . . . we were worried about you. Let me take you home."

"I don't want to go home."

"I'm sorry, Libby." Katie caught up with us. She hugged her sister.

I stooped down to face Libby and took her hands. "Libby. The next time you feel like running away . . . run away to my house."

And she did. That was the beginning of

years of running away to my house, sometimes in tears. We'd sit in the living room, and she'd tell me what made her angry or sad.

"My friend has a godmother," she told me one day. "Will you be my godmother?"

My heart melted. "Yes, of course."

Neither of us knew what it involved since neither of our families had godparents. But we both knew it was a special promise to each other.

Later, when Big Ben sounded, I was ready to drop what I was doing and see what was in store for that day. Every time we said good-bye we'd hug.

"You're almost as tall as me," I told her.

"I'm only to your shoulder, but I'll be to your chin soon."

It wouldn't be hard for her to accomplish that goal; I'm only five feet tall.

"I'm to your chin!" she exclaimed one day. "I'll be taller than you!"

In time we were looking eye to eye. Before I realized it she was looking down at me. She'd achieved her goal.

Our times together included visits to our local ice cream store and playing games. Our favorite was the board game Sorry, which we played at lightning speed.

We celebrated holidays together. Christmas and Easter were our favorites. I made her a big Christmas stocking with her favorite animal on it — a pig. Every year I'd get it out and fill it with her favorite candy. We'd shop for Christmas presents for each other on a Saturday, have lunch, then go home and wrap the gifts. A couple of hours later she would come over and we'd have our own celebration with s'mores, hot chocolate, and a present exchange.

On Easter I would fill an Easter basket and hide it in the living room for her to find. Then we'd take turns hiding the plastic candy-filled eggs.

Each year she became busier with school, friends, and family. Instead of seeing her every day or every afternoon, I might see her once a week or less. We arranged special times together. We drove to a Maine beach where she swam in ice-cold water, loving every minute, while I shivered waiting on the beach. Another time we went to Maine to explore an old fort and ate ice cream sundaes at the Goldenrod in York Beach.

Other special times happened in my home.

"Mrs. Perkins, can we make a meal together and dress up like we're going to a fancy dinner?"

What wonderful ideas she had! We spent the afternoon going over my cookbooks and deciding what to make. On our appointed day, we gathered in my kitchen.

"Here's your apron, Libby." She slipped the navy-blue-and-white-striped apron over her head. I grabbed my red-and-white-striped apron, and we went to work.

"I want to make the dessert," she insisted. I started on the main course.

Libby set out the dishes on my lace tablecloth, put candles at the ends of the table, and arranged black-eyed Susans in a vase.

"It's time to dress," I told her.

"I'll be back in a few minutes," she called as she hurried out the kitchen door. I changed into an ivory lace dress, draped long white beads around my neck, and found my vintage fan. She returned wearing a simple white slip dress and pink necklace.

I fluttered my fan. "Won't you please be seated, my dear?"

She accepted with upturned chin and a twist of her head. "Thank you."

It was one of the most elegant meals I've ever experienced.

Not long after our wonderful meal, Libby came over with another idea. She carried an armload of old clothes, fabric, and a piece of paper with a sketch of a skirt.

"Can you help me make this skirt?" She pointed to the picture. "We can cut up any of these old clothes."

"Did you draw that?"

"Uh-huh. I want one just like my design."

"Without a pattern?" I was being stretched once again.

"Sure!"

Her can-do attitude challenged me. I found some newsprint and we drew her skirt to size on the paper. Soon she was cutting fabric and I was sewing. She went home that day wearing the skirt of her vision.

When Libby went to college her family moved away. I wouldn't see a barefoot girl come through the trees anymore. Her visits became infrequent. If she was home for vacation and didn't come over, I was disappointed. At times I was tempted to call her and say, "Will you play with me?"

Recently I dashed around the house straightening the clutter and clearing the game table. Pulling out the old Sorry game box, I gazed at the now-dull yellow cover, smudged from grubby hands, its corners held together with tape. Inside the box, all the game pieces were accounted for. I laid it on the table. Nearly a year had passed since I'd seen her.

I waited with excited expectation. I jumped when the bell rang and ran up the stairs. Flinging open the door, I know I wore a silly smile, but I couldn't help it. I looked at her with so much love. How beautiful she looked in her simple sundress and her long brown hair. She was now a head taller than I.

"Hi, Libby!"

"Hey, Mrs. Perkins!"

We hugged, and I led my twenty-one-year-old goddaughter downstairs for a special time of sharing . . . and a game of Sorry.

— *Laurie A. Perkins*

Sometimes love comes in unexpected packages, at surprising places, and even at inconvenient times. We might be tempted to respond with impatience, frustration, and even rudeness. But those aren't the responses of a caring heart.

As Laurie discovered, perhaps one of the keys to finding an enduring affection is to just be willing . . . willing to accept the interruptions and intrusions. As we keep our minds — and hearts — open to relationship possibilities, we might receive gifts and blessings that we never dreamed attainable. Who knows? We might even discover that our lives have been delightfully changed.

OPPOSITES ATTRACT — THEN WHAT?

My husband admits that he started doubting our marriage as early as the limo ride from the wedding to the reception. Our driver decided to take the scenic route to the country club and I was furious, worrying about our guests who were waiting to eat.

During what should have been one of the happiest moments of my life, I was on an emotional roller-coaster ride that my new husband was desperately trying to fix. Clay, always calm and level-headed, encouraged me to relax, but my redhead temper was uncontrollable at that point.

In fact, Clay and I spent a lot of time during our first year of marriage trying to manipulate each other to act and react in the ways we deemed appropriate. Clay needed me to be more rational, while I wished he were more open-minded and spontaneous. Maybe it's true that opposites attract, but what should they do after they get married?

I am a fiery Irish gal, who was reared by an opinionated mother and an adoring father. Our family gatherings consisted of lively debates. All the grandkids, cousins, and friends filled the house with laughter and loud discussion. Then there was the grand finale of singing around the piano until three in the morning.

On the other hand, Clay's family is much more structured. His parents are polite and courteous, and Clay was taught to be respectful at all times. They are sensible, logical, early-to-bed, early-to-rise, healthy, wealthy, and wise people.

During our courtship, Clay was enamored by my creativity and drive. He was attracted to my positive attitude and appreciated the fact that I always saw the best in him. Conversely, I was impressed with Clay's intelligence and gentle demeanor. He was the kind of person I could trust completely, and I felt a sense of stability when I was with him. It seemed like a match made in heaven.

Those quirky differences that attracted us during our courtship turned into sources of stress during the early days of our marriage. I remember a huge blowup that started over the remote control. In Clay's family, his dad was the Almighty King of the Remote Control. All the kids and grandkids knew if Granddaddy was watching television, they were to be well-mannered and watch what he was watching.

In my family, everyone would fight over what to watch and the loudest person usually won. Mom argued in favor of political news, Dad wanted to watch sports, my brother and I begged to watch sitcoms. On any given night, one family member could win the shouting match for control of the television.

After being married only two months, I started to notice that Clay controlled the television and I did not think it was fair. So what did I do? I stated my case for the remote that night. "This is my favorite show, it only comes on once a week, and I haven't seen it since we got married!"

Clay calmly responded that the Braves were playing, and he went back to watching the game. He had no idea of the fury that was about to be unleashed on him at that moment. I have been a part of some very serious shouting matches in my family and had learned from the best. I gave a roaring speech, complete with the heart and passion of a political candidate on the day before an election.

Clay just sat in utter shock, blindsided by my attack. He was not accustomed to this kind of communication. He felt like this kind of emotional outburst was not necessary. I responded to him with a line from *Jerry Maguire,* saying, "You think we're fighting; I think we're finally talking!"

Our patterns of communication were so different that we weren't sure how to move forward in the marriage.

Thankfully Clay and I had a few important traits in common. We were both extremely determined to enjoy a long, fulfilling marriage, and we were tenacious about pursuing it. We read every marriage book available. We made a decision not to change each other but instead to seek understanding. It didn't happen overnight, but we started to value each other and appreciate how God made us.

What Carl Gustav Jung said is true: "Everything that irritates us about others can lead us to a better understanding of ourselves." As Clay and I struggled to identify with each other, we developed a strong sense of ourselves and our strengths.

We took tests like the Myers-Briggs Personality Type Test, Spiritual Gifts Test, and Love Languages Test in an effort to appreciate our own and the other's strengths. In the process of examining our differences, we discovered more about our personal purpose in life. Surprisingly we also found a lot of common ground. We both love to teach and have a passion for learning. We are both extroverted and look forward to meeting new people in a variety of settings. We have different spiritual gifts, but we are both enthusiastic about international mission trips and have since traveled together to three countries to build houses and teach English.

I don't think this level of success would have been possible without the help of the many books, CDs, and seminars we incorporated from day one. I can remember sitting in a bookstore with Clay, drinking coffee and skimming through stacks of books on relationships. He would look up from his reading and share a quote from Dr. John Gottman. Then I might find an interesting story in Dr. Phil's book, read it to Clay, and discuss it for a few minutes. It was a cheap way to have a date and learn something in the process!

While reading case studies written by experts, Clay and I were happy to find out that our situation was not uncommon. We are not the first man and woman to come from different family backgrounds. We felt comfortable knowing that we were normal and we could get through this. It would have been a mistake to fumble around in the dark, trying to find all the answers on our own when they are already out there for the taking.

I am convinced that no matter how different two people are they can learn to love, appreciate, and communicate with each other on every level if they will take the time to learn about themselves and their partner. The differences between husband and wife certainly set the stage for amusing daytime television drama, but they also provide an opportunity for personal growth and self-awareness.

— *Emily Osburne*

Do you have relationship challenges?

The wisest man who ever lived before Jesus' time, King Solomon, pointed out that nothing under the sun is truly new (see Ecclesiastes 1:9).

And actually, that's true in relationships, too.

Sometimes when we're embroiled in the problems and emotions of being close to another person, we begin to feel as if we're the only ones who've ever gone through this problem, faced this challenge, or endured this experience.

When Emily and Clay began looking outside themselves and checked other resources, they learned that what they were experiencing — the challenges they thought were so un-usual — were actually quite common.

Checking resources means being willing to be teachable — being willing to admit there might be a better way, and being open to listen to the advice of others, whether through counseling, books, or seminars.

When we move outside of our struggles and begin to seek help, we so often find that many people have faced the same issues — and made it through them. And we learn that we can make it, too.

THE NEW
LOVE-ROOM

Friday night! Date night! Movies, eating out, and spending time together.

"Wow, how our Friday nights have changed," I mumbled as I slid a book in the library return slot and walked toward the car.

I opened the door and plopped in the driver's seat, shutting out the cold November wind. I leaned over and kissed my constant companion, my cancer-ridden husband, who had completed another day of chemotherapy. As I turned the ignition key, he said in a low voice, "Honey, I've been thinking. If I don't make it through this, I want you to go on living. Find a nice man and remarry, a nice man like Bob."

"Please don't talk like that," I snapped. "I love you with all my heart and there will never be anyone else for me."

"You're too young to live the rest of your life —" he started.

"Stop!" I shouted as I gulped back the tears. "I've loved you since high school, and I could never love anyone else. No more talk like this, please?"

I knew why his thoughts had wandered in this scary direction. Several hours earlier, we'd talked with our friends Betty and Bob. Betty was in the final stages of ovarian cancer and we all felt the heavy cloud of death hanging over our heads. The dark cloud had hung over Betty's life for three years. And now my husband, Richard, was diagnosed with stage-four colon cancer. Now we, too, lived in the same unwanted place of darkness and despair.

The friendship and love we four shared were like rays of sunshine peeking through the dark clouds of our lives. However, I did not want to discuss any future that did not include the love of my life, my best friend, and my husband of forty-six years.

Two months later I was forced to face that future. Richard died. It was like most of me had been amputated without anesthesia — except for a broken heart still beating within me and filled with love for the same person.

Desperate for help, I joined a grief support group that included Bob and another woman who had recently lost her spouse. We shared our pain, cried, and walked the path of grief together. After many months, we tiptoed back into the world of intermittent laughter and fun. We three shared a bond, a special friendship, and a comfort that allowed us to step out in new directions.

"I miss my old golfin' buddy," Bob mentioned one day. "Any chance you'd go out and play with me sometime?"

"Okay, let's give it a try," I said.

Bob's compliments and enthusiasm for my game raised my spirits, and we frequently played together.

One night Bob picked me up at the airport when I returned from a trip, and when I opened the car door I found a single yellow rose on the passenger's seat.

"What is this?" I asked.

"Well, I've missed you and wanted to welcome you home," he commented. "Can I buy you dinner?"

What a caring, kind gentleman, I thought. Our conversation that night regarding our future pushed me in a new direction. We began spending more time together, getting to know each other as individuals instead of as grieving friends. One evening several months later, Bob rather casually said, "You know I love you."

Startled, I thought, *Love! What does that*

mean? Both he and I had often referred to our deceased spouses as the love of our life. I knew beyond a shadow of a doubt that I loved Richard with all of my heart, in my very soul, so what would it mean to say "I love you" to someone else? The No Vacancy sign I'd hung on my heart stopped me from responding to Bob. But I asked myself again and again for many days, weeks, and months what it would mean to say "I love you" to someone else.

One time when Bob brought up the subject of love again, I confessed my confusion, and he responded, "At our age, love is different than it was when we were teenagers or in our early twenties."

"It was giggles, excitement, and I-have-to-spend-every-moment-with-you," I remembered.

"I believe there is also a mature love for mature people," he continued with a smile. "It doesn't diminish the love we felt for Betty or Richard. I believe it enhances it. It still means I want to spend time with you, and it's saying yes to a future with hope."

I discussed it with a close friend.

"Your heart is big enough for more than one love," she explained. "Think how much you love your children, grandchildren, and friends. It's like God keeps adding on rooms in your heart for new loves."

I could understand and accept that answer. A sense of peace filled my being. And the next time Bob whispered "I love you," I whispered back "I love you, too."

That was four years ago. Like the yellow rose Bob gave me that memorable evening, our feelings for each other began opening into a lovely bloom. Before we were married, we each honestly expressed our priorities of faith and family.

"It's so good to see you both laughing and happy again," our children unanimously agreed, blessing our relationship.

The foundation of our marriage was a mature love, a comfortable companionship, a trust in each other, a unique bond of shared grief, and a belief that we were doing God's will. We were building a second story onto the rambling ranch house of our previous lives.

Not forgetting our past experiences, we focused on being thankful for good marriages, understanding families, and the wisdom we had learned over the years.

The new love-room in my heart has expanded as we have tried new adventures. Whether it's going on golf trips with friends from my old life or taking a cruise with Bob and Betty's friends, when we extend ourselves for one another, that room in my heart warms.

Recently I was away for a long weekend with some friends, and my eight-year-old granddaughter, Annabelle, told her mother, "Since Nana's gone tonight, I'll bet Mr. Bob sure misses her."

My daughter replied, "You know, Mr. Bob was alone after he lost his wife just like Nana was alone when she lost your grandfather."

After a few minutes, logical Annabelle asked, "When you lose someone, does everyone try to find someone else who is alone and has lost someone?"

"Well, if it works out to find someone you care about and grow to love, then you're pretty blessed," her mother said.

"I'm glad we found Mr. Bob," Annabelle concluded.

I am too, Annabelle. I am too.

— *Betty J. Johnson Dalrymple*

Since love is one of the most exhilarating experiences a human can have, losing it is one of the most painful experiences. So many times, like Betty, when we've faced the pain of a lost love, we hang out a No Vacancy sign — unwilling to allow the risk of another loss in our lives. The numb pain of grief seems somehow safer than the potential hurt we just might experience if we make room in our hearts for someone else.

Aren't you glad that our capacity to love isn't limited? What a shame to sit uncomfortably in an emotional one-room shack, when we could enjoy a mansion. As long as we're willing to take a chance, our room for love can grow and grow.

Adding rooms to the home in our hearts may cost us at times — we may have to get used to a new way of life, or learn to trust again, or risk losing again. But the result well exceeds the construction expenses.

A CHRISTMAS
MIRACLE

I thought I had the inside scoop on loving and forgiving and living a happy, carefree life. But then my granddaughter Ashley was victimized by my youngest son, Daniel.

When I learned this, the pain plunged me into a whirlwind of confused emotions. My happy, loving family was instantly engaged in an enraged battle. Police reports were filed. Family communications halted. Love and trust turned into anger and accusations. The family bond I cherished now hung by a thread. Everyone was distraught.

In the midst of their anger, my granddaughter's parents, Paul, my oldest son, and his wife, Claudia, gave me an ultimatum. They wanted me to disown Daniel and only extend love to the rest of my devastated family; or I could continue my relationship with Daniel and relinquish all rights of ever seeing Ashley and my other granddaughters again. They felt Daniel should be stripped of love and excommunicated from the family. And I was expected to forget he existed.

How could anyone tell me to disown my own child or expect me to give up my grandchildren? I was being forced to decide which family member deserved the most love. I was overcome with grief because I loved all of them.

How could I possibly choose between any of them? I knew that no matter what I decided, I had no promise of my family ever regaining the bonds of love and happiness we had once held so dear.

I chose to remain neutral in this terrible situation, but since Daniel still lived at home, I made the painful decision to put him out of my house. My heart was torn as I watched him walk away. But I knew I could not put my grandchildren at risk of falling prey to Daniel's addiction.

Daniel began living on the streets, and the police had to pick him up for questioning. Then after hours of interrogation they let him go because they didn't have any evidence to convict him. He was thrust back into his own world of survival filled with rejection, rebellion, and anger.

I thought I would die of a broken heart. I cried out to God. Then I screamed at God, "How could my child do such a horrible thing? This is not supposed to happen in my family. What happened to our love?"

I began wallowing in a quagmire of self-pity and shame over Daniel's actions.

To make matters worse, the rest of my family withdrew from me. I couldn't understand anyone purposely rejecting a family member and deeming him unworthy of love, regardless of the crime. I could understand my family being enraged at Daniel, but to be stripped of love was too painful for me to imagine.

Paul and Claudia shut me out of their lives. They refused to let me talk to my granddaughters since I refused to disown Daniel. They felt I had abandoned them and was overlooking the crime he had committed.

As the months passed, I became consumed with the hostility and uncertainties my family was suffering. After many restless nights of constant turmoil, I hesitantly began journaling my confused emotions. At first I drew circles while my thoughts spun in my head. Words slowly began to appear on the scribbled sheets until my thoughts and feelings spilled out.

As I wrote about the pain of my divided family, I realized that writing about it was therapeutic. I began to imagine myself in

Paul and Claudia's position as parents of a molested child. Writing how I thought they felt opened my eyes and helped me to better understand their torment.

I discovered that through this release of writing, selfishness, self-pity, shame, and depression were replaced with a renewed understanding of unconditional love. I began to entertain renewed hope for restoration.

Overlooking my own pain forced me to quit focusing on myself. It caused me to evaluate my family's actions. I chose to reevaluate the past few months, listen to my heart, and be the loving mother I had been before. I had to decide to overlook all the harsh words that had been spoken and forgive everyone, including Daniel.

In making the right choices, I knew I had to take the first step toward communication. I began calling Paul and Claudia. At first they were curt with me on the phone. When I tried to visit they wouldn't allow me inside their home, but I persisted in my attempts to extend love and understanding to them. I refused to give up regardless of their anger.

After several weeks, Paul and Claudia began reciprocating my efforts to communicate. Our visits were short and sweet.

We avoided any discussion of our family division. I didn't know if the tension had really subsided or if it was just lying dormant, waiting to erupt.

Then Claudia called one day and asked if she could come visit me. After she arrived we talked about the weather, the granddaughters' school, and what was for dinner, purposely avoiding any controversial subject. Later, I nervously mentioned that writing in my journal had helped me overcome so many painful hurdles.

Surprised that I would actually document the horrible crime, Claudia asked to read my journal. I was just as surprised at her request, but allowed her to delve into my most personal notes. My stomach was in knots as she sat quietly soaking in every word. I didn't interrupt when I peeked in on her because I was afraid she would be angry with me. However, I was shocked to see tears rolling down her cheeks as she read.

When she finally finished reading, she came into the kitchen where I was trying to keep busy. She walked straight to me, hugged me, buried her face on my shoulder, and wept.

Claudia said she was awed by my perception of her pain. She realized our suffering was similar, but we had been unable to communicate. She apologized for her part in the family's division.

I was shocked at her response to my journal notes. We expressed our love for each other and wept together over all that had happened. We discovered that without love in our family, we were all miserable.

Claudia insisted that Paul read the journal. Before long every family member had read about my broken heart from the pages of that journal. Who could have imagined that this release from pain would open the door of restoration in my family?

My family was reunited, except for Daniel. Now Paul, Claudia, and the granddaughters visit often. My home is filled with laughter and love once again. We learned the hard way that without love, life smothers any hope of ever finding happiness.

Since I knew Daniel felt rejected and unloved when I asked him to leave my home, I had to track him down to let him know how much I loved him, even though I didn't condone his actions or approve of his lifestyle. He is my son so loving him comes naturally. But I made a conscious choice to forgive him and to extend unconditional love to him.

Dreams of always having my family gather

on special holidays and family reunions were destroyed by Daniel's behavior. But this renewed strength to fight for my family birthed a new hope of reconciliation in my heart. I wanted to believe that love would prevail and that Daniel would someday be reunited with the entire family.

Standing firm in my love for each family member proved to be rewarding. My sister invited me to her home just two weeks before Christmas. When I arrived, my daughter Shelly was there and she informed me that I must be blindfolded for a surprise.

I tried to figure out what gift they were going to present to me. As the blindfold covered my eyes, I imagined a new car, some outstanding jewelry, or even airline tickets to Hawaii or some remote vacation spot.

I heard shuffling around me as my sister untied the blindfold. All three of my grown children stood before me smiling, with their arms draped around one another.

"Merry Christmas, Mom!" they exclaimed.

I was so overcome with shock, joy, and confusion that I fell to my knees weeping. Paul and Shelly hadn't spoken to Daniel in more than seven years . . . and here they were in the same room, laughing. They kissed me as they handed me a large box.

Opening the gift, I saw several framed pictures of my children. All three of them had met at a park and had pictures taken. It was unbelievable! I was experiencing a real Christmas miracle: Love was being restored.

I am so thankful that I chose to forgive, look beyond my own pain, and focus on my family's pain. My family found a renewed sense of peace and a profound depth of love.
— *Loretta J. Eidson*

Sometimes the situations we face seem hopeless. Relationships seem to be irretrievably damaged. The logical step seems to be to let go of those we once held so dear, grieve our losses, and move on the best we can.

However, Loretta reminds us that as long as we're alive, if we're willing to do the hard work, pray, and forgive, we can often find hope for reconciliation even when the situation seems impossible.

It does take more than one person to make relationships work — we can't guarantee that miracles will happen just because we're willing to work at it. However, sometimes, as Loretta found, the persistent love and communication of one person can break down the walls of pain and misunderstanding and set in motion the wheels of forgiveness and relationship renewal.

Never give up too soon on the people you care about.

Between the Baby
and Basketball

Not long ago I thought I knew what true love and sacrifice were.

After all, I'd had plenty of experience with both. Having endured a broken marriage engagement, I'd learned love couldn't be built on good intentions. It needed stability, responsibility, and sacrifice.

Through dating, I'd compiled a healthy "never do" list, which included but wasn't restricted to: Never leave the toilet seat up; never ask, "Why does your mother always do that?"; and never make specific or indirect references to weight gain.

After marriage, I added several items, including: Never compare your wife's meatballs to your mother's, and never say, "Well, Mom always made it this way. . . ."

Four years into marriage, I'd done pretty well. A mentor had given me the good advice that "love isn't all poems and romance; it's hard work and sacrifice," so I'd worked hard. I shared dishwashing, laundry, and other chores with my wife, made dinner now and then, and even watched a chick flick or two.

I bought and picked flowers, and even worked on her flower gardens one summer as a birthday gift. Everything was great; we were happy and had just welcomed our first child. I knew how to love my wife and how to make sacrifices.

But one night after walking along Route 81, north out of Binghamton, New York, in the rain, I realized I didn't know a thing.

It was my second year coaching men's basketball at Davis College, and the season had fallen apart. I'd made key mistakes and we'd lost games, but worst of all I'd lost the confidence of my players and the fans.

Coaching part time and teaching full time had worn me down, and though wondrous, our daughter's birth had turned our lives upside down. I was fighting too many battles and losing them all. For a while I'd managed to make everything look great on the outside. But one night, walking home in the rain after my truck had a flat tire, I imploded.

We'd lost badly again that afternoon. Our season, which had shown early promise, was disintegrating before my very eyes and I was powerless to stop it. Worse, I'd lost my temper and now players were whispering. I knew my athletic director would eventually hear about the episode.

So as I trudged down a dark, lonely highway in the rain, I worried about these things: our disappointing season, my reputation as a coach and a person, and my tattered plans of basketball success.

Chilled by wind and rain, I couldn't see past the darkness, the black highway asphalt, and my coaching woes. This was my one chance to prove my worth and it was slipping away. Not only would I have questions to answer tomorrow, I'd also need to have my truck towed off the highway and its tire fixed — something we really couldn't afford.

I was glad to reach home. Cold, tired, and discouraged, I wanted to sleep my troubles away so I'd have the energy to fix all these things. But then I opened the front door. My first sight was of my wife, crying and desperate, while my newborn daughter screamed.

My wife, Abby, is a nurse. She's not rattled easily. In her typical day, she deals with gruesome things. But before that night I'd never seen her so upset and afraid.

My world telescoped. Everything "important" dropped away, leaving only my crying, frightened wife and my wailing baby girl.

The problem turned out to be something minor. Madison had suffered her first cold and couldn't breathe well. We were new, anxious parents, easily scared. However, the incident hit me like a sledgehammer.

Later that night, I realized I'd gone the whole day without thinking of Abby or Madison, my mind occupied by such big, important things. During my lonely sojourn down Route 81, I'd obsessed over my basketball troubles, while my wife worried about our daughter's well-being, desperate for my return.

Some might say that night was just part of the normal challenges in balancing coaching and raising a family. Regardless, it signaled the end of my coaching career. For the first time in a while, I asked Abby, "What do you need most from me right now?" We talked until three in the morning.

Two weeks later my coaching career ended, well before the season did. Perhaps my departure was hasty, maybe even acrimonious. Certainly many were confused, concerned, let down . . . possibly even hurt. I fielded phone calls and e-mails from parents, friends, and associates, explaining as best I could. Eventually I simply told everyone, "My family needs me more than Davis College basketball does."

It was true. When I finished coaching the stress faded. Our lives became our own again and a very simple, pleasant routine emerged: I went to school, taught, and came home to my wife and daughter.

I'd finally discovered what it meant to truly love through my difficult career sacrifice.

Hadn't I?

One last bump in the road remained. Several weeks after I left the court for the last time, my wife was scheduled for her first weekend of work back at the hospital.

With shortness of breath, sweaty palms, and clenching heart, I thought, *This isn't good!*

I was a guy; guys didn't watch babies. They fixed things, took out the garbage, mowed lawns. They didn't watch babies. Plus I was perhaps the clumsiest man on earth. I dropped and broke things. I wasn't good at following directions and had a short attention span. What if I mixed her formula wrong or she suffocated under her blanket when I wasn't paying attention?

Also the thought of her crying intimidated me. I'm not violent, but I'd heard about parents who panicked with crying kids and accidentally hurt the fragile babies.

Plus I had my own hobbies that I only had time to pursue on the weekends. Hadn't I sacrificed enough? Did I have to give up my spare time too?

The week before my date with baby-sitting destiny — or doom, depending on whom you spoke to — I peppered my wife with these doubts. I thought of ways we could keep her home from work just a little while longer until we could afford a baby-sitter. I made rational arguments about how Madison would benefit if Abby stayed home longer. Right up until that fateful Saturday morning, I badgered and poked and prodded. Then once again my life telescoped and I got a hard, unflattering look at myself.

Here was Abby dressed for work, tears in her eyes at the thought of leaving her firstborn. Not only did she worry about that but she also worried about how she'd perform at work. Could she keep up? Was she ready physically? She, better than I, understood our finances and knew she needed to work, but she was torn.

At that moment when my wife needed her husband's support, what was I doing to help her?

Nothing! I'd only made her feel worse in the hope that she'd stay home so I could duck the responsibility of caring for Madison.

In that moment I realized something shocking: Through all the turbulence of the past few months I'd learned nothing. I was still doing what I wanted to do.

I realized an awful truth about my resignation: Coaching had become a burden. I was tired physically, emotionally, and spiritually. Things hadn't worked out the way anyone wanted, and I hadn't wanted to coach anymore.

Don't misunderstand. Leaving basketball behind was necessary. Our lives improved drastically once I quit coaching. However, in the end, I quit because I didn't want to do it anymore.

That Saturday morning I learned a lesson of love. Love requires hard work and sacrifice; but so often it requires sacrifices we don't want to make at all — in fact, are scared witless to make.

I'd tricked myself into thinking my resignation was the ultimate sacrifice because, after all, I loved basketball. Walking away from coaching had been hard, but I'd missed the subtle fact that I wanted to walk away.

In contrast, truly loving someone might require our doing what we fear most and want to do the *least.* Unfortunately, we often deceive ourselves about how sacrificial we really are.

With a deep breath, I told my wife, "Go to work, honey. We'll be okay."

Blinking back tears, she whispered, "Are you sure?"

I nodded and grinned. "We'll manage. You need to do this, but honestly . . . so do I."

That weekend I also learned about an entirely different type of love. For two days this lovely baby girl's welfare was completely in my hands. At two months old she was powerless. In this case, showing true love meant holding the very essence of life in my hands and providing for her every need, every moment. For two days I existed completely in a sacrificial moment — sometimes unwillingly (like when I wanted to nap and she didn't) — in order to preserve my daughter's life.

I'd like to paint a warm rendition of tenderness and intimate father-daughter moments. Yes, those moments did occur. However, I mostly remember baptism by every bodily fluid known to man. I also spent nine hours both days in the same rocking chair because I discovered that when Madison fell asleep, we were both better off if I just stayed there. I learned that though babies certainly know when they're hungry, they don't always know when they're full. You can imagine the results if they're not burped regularly.

My life changed forever that weekend. I'm human, so I still make mistakes more often than I'd like. However, today I enjoy a close relationship with my daughter and my son, because I've labored in this selfless love. Our marriage has been blessed because Abby knows that instead of just doing the "man stuff," I've come alongside her, taken her hand, and walked with her on our journey.

That's what true sacrifice is, and what leads to true love. Love's lessons are never over, nor are we ever done making sacrifices. We do so in small, day-to-day moments for the rest of our lives.

— *Kevin Lucia*

So many times we call something "sacrifice" when, as in Kevin's situation, it's something we really wanted to do anyway. When we do this, we only fool ourselves. Those we love certainly know the truth. And then we wonder why they're not impressed with our actions.

As Kevin points out, when we love, sacrifice becomes a way of life. That kind of selflessness isn't found in the large, grandiose, life-changing gestures. Instead, it's found in the small daily choices. It's revealed in the times when we put our own desires aside for someone else. That's the way we show we really care. And those little selfless moments are the ones that truly bless and impress.

A Reason to Live

The knock on my door was persistent. When I opened the door, a tired-looking, thin, gaunt-faced figure with disheveled hair stared at me. Her clothes hung from her body, and she defiantly scowled. She seemed to be in her early twenties. Beside her stood a woman I barely recognized: Mitty, an old acquaintance I hadn't seen in sixteen years.

After the women settled on the living room sofa, Mitty said she was now living in a city sixty-five kilometers from my town. Somehow she had found me. Mitty revealed that the woman with her, Mona, her younger sister — who sat passively and stared at her toes — had attempted suicide a few days earlier. Mona had consumed insecticide but had survived. Mitty told me she now spoke to no one and refused to eat.

Mitty left after an hour. To my shock, she walked out without Mona. I assumed she would come back and take Mona home. But

116

hours passed and Mitty didn't return. The hours turned into days. Mitty never returned for Mona.

I was not prepared for this shock. I was too stunned to even think. In my town in India we didn't have a crisis center or a suicide intervention program or a women's shelter or even Alcoholics Anonymous or a psychiatrist. What on earth — or rather, what in heaven — was I going to do?

I was neck-deep in several projects. One project required me to commute by train and bus to another city for four hours each day. I was working twelve hours a day, six days a week. I didn't have time for Mona. What was I to do with this total stranger I'd never seen or met before — a woman her own family didn't want.

I had no extra room in the house, so I settled Mona near the window in my room, setting up a folding bed and a chair and small table.

"Would you like some coffee?" I asked gently. She said nothing, but collapsed onto the bed. She stayed there for a week, seldom moving, staring at the ceiling with dead, vacant eyes. Each day I coaxed her to at least take some fruit juice.

She gulped it wordlessly. The icy walls she'd built around her were impenetrable.

It seemed she was frustrated about having survived the suicide attempt and had resolved to slowly starve herself to death. She urgently needed nourishment. But she balked at the slightest suggestion of a sandwich, popcorn, ice cream, or even my delicious Tandoori chicken I thought no one could resist.

I was too tired to converse after work and making dinner every evening, but I kept urging her to sample some soup. Finally one evening she reluctantly ate some, probably so I would quit bothering her!

How can a person who has no hunger for life itself feel any physical hunger? I wondered.

Her stony silence and angry brow betrayed bottled-up hatred. Deep rejection, hopelessness, and heavy despair seemed to have enveloped her completely.

I had no idea if she'd ever speak, but still, one weekend I asked, "Would you like to talk about what has been bothering you? I want to help you if you'll let me. I care. I'm not here to judge you, but to listen to what you have to say. To understand why you feel your life isn't worth living."

She looked at me blankly, hesitantly. I wondered if she would find the courage. I didn't push her, but continued to care. As the days passed, I talked to her even if she didn't respond. One winter afternoon she let me take her into the garden for a walk. I watered the plants and she sat on a fallen log. I prayed that nature's soothing influence would help, that the warm sunbeams would thaw even a small part of her frozen heart.

Another day I took her for an outing, and when we returned, she actually ate some curried rice. For a few moments she even played with my puppy, whom she had ignored every day.

Weeks went by and then suddenly, on one of my rare days off, she dared to reveal the pieces of her shattered self. She said she wished she hadn't been born, for she was unwanted like the rest of her many sisters. Her father, angry at having no sons, was a hate-filled, abusive man who had unleashed his disgust and fury upon her.

Mona had often stood up to his insults, ridicule, and humiliation when no one else would dare. The two would have terrible shouting matches. When he'd scream, "You're good for nothing!" she'd scream back, "Just like you!"

Her mother, a kind, simple housewife, accepted her husband's abuse. Mona's older sisters had all married and she was one of the last left home, the wild one her angry father couldn't subdue. To escape his wrath, she often ran away from home. She got involved with a bad crowd, with drugs and alcohol.

No one had ever taken her for counseling. Her siblings wanted nothing to do with her. Her mother loved her and urged her to make a better life for herself. But though the drugs were ruining her intelligent mind and the alcohol was enslaving her, she couldn't quit. She didn't care. She had come to a dead end.

I didn't know how I was supposed to grasp all this and deal with someone I didn't even know. How was I to spark her will to live when she wished to die? How could I help someone who felt only hatred and anger toward herself, her family, the world, and especially me for trying to make her live? How could I love such an unlovable, self-destructive person? How long was I to shelter her?

At first this emaciated skeleton seemed quiet and simply passive. But as she felt stronger her bitter rage returned. Mona would keep running off and then returning. And I would pray that the Lord would somehow guide her steps back home.

One evening Mona left a note on my desk

saying she couldn't live anymore.

Where would I even begin searching for someone who didn't want to be found? As I had done so many times since Mona entered my life, I knelt in prayer and desperately asked God to hold on to her. She returned after forty-eight agonizing hours, her clothes caked in mud.

She told me she had walked into the dark night to a huge water reservoir near the outskirts of town. She had planned to drown herself but couldn't. I made her coffee and listened, trembling from relief.

I tried to take her to a psychologist in a nearby city. It took two weeks to talk her into it. My mother located one of Mona's sisters and asked her to accompany Mona when I took her to the psychologist, but the sister refused. Although Mitty had been a nurse for years, she informed me that Mona wasn't her problem anymore.

Not one of Mona's sisters would be responsible or even supportive while I was trying so hard to help her get back on her feet. What terrible rejection for Mona! How disappointing to realize they just didn't care about my efforts to help their sister.

So I drove Mona seventy kilometers on my scooter to meet with the psychologist three times a week. And once there, Mona refused to answer a single question. After many appointments, she finally began talking.

Just when she seemed to be progressing well she suddenly refused to return for therapy.

The situation intensified. One afternoon she tried to set herself on fire after finding kerosene in my storeroom. She stood in the middle of the kitchen, kerosene-soaked and holding matches, cursing and targeting her anger on me.

I begged God to help me stop her. Never had I been in such a situation. I wrestled as never before, and somehow wrenched the matchbox away.

"Why don't you let me die, you fool?" she thundered. "It's my life!"

Finally she collapsed in sobs. I rushed her to the hospital, where she stayed a few days. Of course, no one came to pick her up, though three of her sisters knew about the hospitalization. Again, with great dread, I prepared to take her home.

I decided I would try one last time. If she resumed therapy, stuck to it, and proved she was serious, I would help her.

My mother and I prayed for her, over her, and with her. And one night I read aloud my favorite psalm, Psalm 91: "Those who live in the shelter of the Most High will find rest in the shadow of the Almighty. This I declare about the Lord: He alone is my refuge, my place of safety; he is my God, and I trust him" (vv. 1–2).

She actually listened. Intently.

A few weeks later I read Philippians 4:13, "For I can do everything through Christ, who gives me strength."

I told her that she had to give up her addictions and go for therapy. She didn't say a word, but I knew she was thinking seriously about it.

During our next discussion, Mona told me she had never known or needed or heeded God.

"There is no God, and even if there is, He doesn't care. No one cares," she insisted.

"He cared enough to bring you to my door," I countered. "Did I not care? Did I turn you away?"

This time she did not hold her tears back. She let them flow freely all night. At dawn I asked the Lord to take control of her spirit, mind, and body . . . her life.

For once she bowed her head with me in prayer — to a God she never thought existed.

A healing process began very slowly. She started to eat and sleep well. She did triumph over the alcohol and the drugs after more than a year of intense struggle.

One day I took her home to her family. They were stunned to see her. Her mother gaped in disbelief.

Over the next two years Mona came and went. She talked about the difference Jesus was making in her life, and how tough it was trying to cope with a new lifestyle — one that involved self-discipline. She liked Psalm 121:3: "He will not let you stumble; the one who watches over you will not slumber."

Three long years later she finally was able to keep a job.

Helping someone in such great need, in such dire circumstances, made me rely heavily on God's love, wisdom, and guidance.

I had never looked after anyone in that way. The challenge of being there to show love in the face of rejection, to be patient through the unbearable temptation of giving up, to stay up night after night worrying and praying was too much.

As days turned to weeks and months, only by God's absolute grace could I show love, acceptance, and support.

Seven years have gone by since that unexpected knock on my door. How hard it was for me to give my time, help, and understanding to just one person! But God is available for all of His own children across the world, anytime, always.

When I awake in the middle of the night, I know He will be unfailingly there. How blessed I am to reach for His comforting and constant presence! I do not take that gift and privilege for granted anymore.

— *Sudha Khristmukti*

Thankfully most of us will never have to face a situation anywhere near as dramatic or unusual as Sudha faced. However, many of us may need to deal with those who are angry, suicidal, or addictive.

Thankfully most of us also have resources to help us as we help desperate people. However, even with resources, difficult people take time, energy, and every bit of fortitude we have.

Sudha accepted the challenge to love someone who was not only a stranger to her but one who also resented Sudha's caring for her. Maybe in some ways we're not so unlike Sudha. Pain or addictions can turn anyone we love into a stranger. And people in pain turn their hurt, frustration, and anger on those of us who are brave enough or caring enough to approach them.

How do we love such people? Sometimes, as Sudha learned, the first step is accepting them where they are: nurturing them and trying to take care of their basic needs while they start to find life again. Patience as they start to mentally process their situation. Not taking it personally when they lash out in pain. Helping them get to resources that will help them help themselves. Being prepared for the ups and downs of recovery.

Love is stubborn. And as Sudha expresses, we can only find love strong enough for the addictive or angry person by the grace of God.

BETTER THAN
CHOCOLATE

How do we measure love? Once upon a time I measured it by a heart-shaped box of chocolates.

When I was a child, Valentine's Day was one of the most important days of the year. Certain things were a tradition on Valentine's Day. We had a party at school: Everyone gave everyone else cards, and we had plenty of cupcakes and candy. And my dad always gave my mom a box of chocolates.

After Mom opened her candy, she let each of us six children have one piece. That was enough for us. What a treat! I looked forward to the day when I, too, would receive chocolates from my husband on Valentine's Day.

The first time my husband, Keith, and I celebrated Valentine's Day after our marriage, he kissed me and left for work as he did every day. But I knew this day would be different. When he came home he would bring that lovely box of chocolates.

To my surprise he arrived home with nothing in his hands. I decided my gift was in the car.

Keith took me to a fast-food place for dinner — still no box of candy. While in the car I peeked in the backseat. Nothing was there.

When we came home Keith didn't mention Valentine's Day. I was annoyed. How could he forget such an important event?

"What's wrong?" he asked, noting my attitude.

"You should know," I responded. Then I gave him the silent treatment.

Of course, I hadn't bought him any chocolates, either. But Dad had always been the one to buy them, not Mom.

Three Valentine's Days later, I still had no chocolates. But by this time I had a list a mile long of things that would improve our marriage. I hated it when he ate potato chips in bed, and the fact that he knew the make of every car on the road and thought everyone else should know as well. He'd quiz me whenever we were out: "Do you know what kind of car that is?"

I soon knew the difference between Fords and Chevys and what year they were made.

It took me a long time to figure out that Keith was looking for validation. He didn't want me to come up with the correct answer. He wanted me to say, "Wow, that's really good that you know so much about cars."

When he worked on the car, he liked to have me sit and watch. It was his way of saying, "Look at me. I can do something useful and important." I didn't see it at the time because, after all, I was the important one.

When we finally discussed my feelings about Valentine's Day, Keith said, "I don't have to give you candy to prove my love. It doesn't mean anything if a wife has to tell her husband to give her presents."

I thought he was being insensitive. Why couldn't he see things my way? If someone had told me I was the insensitive one, I'm sure I wouldn't have believed it.

This destructive pattern in our life continued until Keith was sent overseas to serve in the war. Our son was born three months before he left. The baby and I moved to an apartment near my parents to await Keith's return.

That year, on a very lonely Valentine's Day, my father brought me a heart-shaped box of chocolates because he assumed Keith did that when he was home. I cried. Dad didn't know it was my first box of Valentine chocolates since I had married. I never told him. I didn't want him to think Keith neglected me.

Surprisingly, the moment I saw the chocolates I knew I'd been clinging to something that had no substance. The blinders of selfishness disappeared. My ideas of romance and what was proper for a husband to do went out the window. Dad's gift opened my eyes to how shallow my perspective was.

I realized I would rather have my good, stable, loving husband by my side, with or without a box of chocolates. My list suddenly changed. Instead of seeing the bothersome bits in our marriage, I thought only of the good things we had together. I recalled how he showed his love in more ways than I could count. I remembered the first year of our marriage when he nursed me through an illness. He forced me to take medicine when I fought it. He worked every day and nursed me all night. Now that's love. Why didn't I see it at the time?

Keith has been a good provider, a good father, and a spiritual leader in our home. What more could a woman want? What I believed comprised a romantic relationship was a product of my imagination. Love cannot be measured by a box of chocolates.

Now that I'm older and wiser, I know it's important to tell Keith my thoughts and let him think about them. I've learned that he doesn't like people to tell him what to do — he wants to come up with the idea himself.

After I told Keith how my father brightened my Valentine's Day while he was gone, Keith came up with "an idea," and now he brings me a heart-shaped box of chocolates on Valentine's Day.

As I look back on our years of marriage, I realize what a good thing I have. That first year I was no bargain. I couldn't boil water — the pan went dry. One night I cooked something the recipe book called spaghetti omelet. I couldn't eat it, but Keith did, and said, "It tastes good."

Keith is not afraid to change a baby's diaper, do the laundry, or cook the meals. In fact, he likes to cook. I'm the envy of my friends. Their husbands wouldn't think of cooking dinner or doing the dishes.

Now when my husband gives me a box of chocolates on Valentine's Day, I am content to know that the man who gives them to me does so because he loves me — not because he has to.

— *Midge DeSart*

■ ■ ■ ■

How do you measure love? Each of us speaks a different love "language." For Midge, chocolates on Valentine's Day indicated that her husband loved her. She expected that gift to reassure her.

Her husband, on the other hand, apparently didn't see the importance of giving gifts as a way to say "I love you." Sounds like he showed his adoration for Midge by serving her — taking care of her physical needs and helping around the house.

He was saying "I love you" by his everyday actions, but Midge was expecting to hear "I love you" in the form of a gift.

How can we learn someone's love language? Sometimes by asking, "What makes you feel really loved?" Another way is to watch a person and see how he or she expresses love to others — and then practice that technique on that person.

Love may be a universal language, but sometimes it sounds and looks different to various people.

Who's Winning the War?

"Why do all our conversations have to end in combat?" John growled. "I just asked where you wanted to go for dinner, not which of us rules the roost. Okay, you don't want to go to Andy's Pub because you're afraid I'll keep you out too late. So what's your choice? Should we go to the Dairy Queen, like good little kids?"

My husband stormed out the door for an evening alone at the pub.

Ouch! Perhaps I was overbearing, but I figured I had as much right to "rule the roost" as John did. And for all four years of our marriage, I'd regularly reminded him of my "rights." Besides, John didn't realize how terrible it was to roll out of bed for a full day's work after only four hours' sleep. When we went to Andy's, we always stayed until the wee hours of the morning.

Life would have been carefree if it weren't for John. Clearly all men were impossible! I felt women were unquestionably superior human beings.

So why had I married John? I fell deliriously in love with the cutest, funniest guy I'd ever met. John could be the most adorable sweetheart. When we were dating, he impressed me with his strange combination of gentlemanly manners and clownish behavior. He'd run to open doors, then bow deeply like the Shakespearean actor he endeavored to become. He treated me with the respect I felt I deserved.

However, shortly after we married, John began drinking, and the adorable sweetheart turned to a monster. I tried to control him — to stop his drinking in order to avoid his monster side. But his behavior only got worse.

Of course I was no angel, but felt my bad behavior was justifiable. After all, I had a monster for a husband! Even though I'd have preferred a stable life with a good man, I'd fallen in love with John. So I attempted to pummel him into the husband I required.

Our closest friends felt it was just a matter of time before we divorced. However, John and I remained together, even when everyone else seemed to be divorcing. Perhaps it was stubbornness on our part — wishing to prove our friends wrong. But something made us determined to stay married. And something made us fear divorce enough to take a closer look at the dynamics of our relationship. I believe that something was true love. When we realized how deeply we loved each other, we began making changes to preserve our marriage.

Lifestyle changes came first. We no longer socialized with friends who were primarily bad influences. Then we quit our high-pressure jobs and moved to a small town.

To my relief, John quit drinking. I also tried to change my behavior, to be more compassionate toward my husband. However, I couldn't seem to get past the idea that our world should revolve around me. Nevertheless, we worked hard to put our quarrelsome past behind us and aim at a "happily ever after." We bought a home and started a family.

Then John experienced health problems. For a short time his vision blurred. After that his legs became numb and moved awkwardly. His stumbling gait caused me to think he'd returned to drinking, but John claimed innocence.

Just before our son was born, John was diagnosed with multiple sclerosis — an incurable disease of the central nervous system. As we were busy trying to turn our lives around, MS threatened to destroy everything we were working to build.

Thankfully our baby, Danny, came into the world strong and healthy. But John was already limping from the onset of gradual paralysis, a sign he had one of the worst and rarest forms of MS. He soon depended on crutches. My heart ached for him, but I was so selfish, I had little capacity to reach out in love. And I had very little time for my husband, since I was now caring for an infant.

In his despair, John returned to drinking. My lighthearted clown became an angry, bitter jester, wanting nothing to do with a life that had turned so sour. In his misery, John hid behind a bottle, lashing out if I tried to console him. I'd retreat, licking my wounds, conscious of my vast inadequacies.

I felt stuck in an impossible situation — caring for both a baby *and* a depressed husband. I couldn't leave John. I realized Danny needed his father, but I possessed no resources to handle such challenges. How could I possibly deal with all this?

While I was on a frantic search for answers, a sweet neighbor named Mary intervened. She suggested I give God a try.

The thought of depending on a Being I couldn't see was unusual for me. However,

I was desperate enough to start reading a Bible Mary slipped into my hands. I'd not been much of a reader, but the book grabbed me and wouldn't let go! It was as if the author knew me, and was reading my thoughts. It seemed to be telling my story. It wasn't a pretty tale. However, I was finally receiving a true perspective of my life — a perspective that made me surrender to God.

As I devoured page after page of Mary's Bible, I was convicted of being just as bad a wife to John as he had been a husband. Perhaps worse! Despite intense embarrassment over my errors, something kept me reading that holy book day and night. It had answers for a heart filled with questions. What have I done wrong? Why do I deserve this? What can I do to help John . . . Danny . . . myself?

Answers would leap off the pages with clarity, even though they weren't necessarily written out word for word. It seemed so crazy. Somehow the solutions were being whispered into my heart.

When I read the line "Love your enemies, do good to those who hate you" (Luke 6:27 NIV), something told me, "This is your battle plan."

I grimaced at the thought as I studied the bitter expression on the face of "my enemy."

As usual, John sat in his chair across the room, drinking, while he glared angrily at a blank wall. Loving him would take far more personal sacrifice than I'd given anyone — ever. Yet as I watched Danny playing quietly at his father's feet, I knew I had to do this. I had to love John despite his anger.

So I prayed — yes, me, the independent, all-knowing woman *prayed* — for the ability to love my husband.

I started cautiously reaching out to John, self-preservation being my sole motive. Sensing my guarded attitude, John lashed back harder than ever. I realized I mustn't show fear, so I prayed again. This time I asked for the strength and courage to win back John's heart. I kept approaching him with love and little kindnesses. At first he continued reacting with anger and suspicion, but I kept reaching out.

Then I felt inspired to start complimenting John for his strengths. I determined to praise him at least once every day. Though he outwardly rejected my praise, after a few weeks I saw a crack in his protective shell. And amazingly, as I heard my own words of praise, I began to appreciate John's strong points. He had exceptional intelligence, an exemplary level of responsibility for our family, and a tender care for the weak.

Despite his inner rage, John never spoke an angry word to Danny. He was gentle toward our son — ready to listen and to help wherever he could.

However, the limitations brought by John's disease left him frustrated as a father, a husband, and a man. In addition, he carried the scars of deep hurts . . . especially from me.

By then, I'd realized how inexcusably horrible I'd been to John. So I couldn't blame him for the problems in our relationship. I'd begun our marriage as a self-absorbed brat. It was shocking to admit that my attitudes about John had actually contributed to his drinking rather than controlling it. The time had come to take my eyes off of me and pour all the love and strength I possessed into healing the damage I'd done. I couldn't do anything to stop the multiple sclerosis, but I could love John despite the disease.

My husband's heart seemed to be crying out for such unconditional love. Though it never came out of his lips, his eyes begged the questions: "Do you still love me even though I can't open doors for you? Will you still love me when this disease robs me of all dignity?" I didn't know if I could face what tomorrow would bring, but I kept praying for strength and wisdom.

It wasn't long before I'd surrounded myself with women of faith like Mary — women who knew how to love their husbands and could teach me how to love John. Soon I sensed changes in me. The selfish brat was gone. In spite of myself, God had made me into a woman of patience, faith, and love — a totally new creation. It was *so* satisfying. And by the simple act of loving John, I watched all his best qualities emerge to shine with a brilliance I'd never known.

It took months of consistent kindness and compassion to make progress toward a healthy relationship. Yet as we moved forward, John quit drinking and his anger faded. My silly clown came back.

As the decades passed, our love grew stronger with every challenge. Our battle with multiple sclerosis continued for thirty years. But since I'd learned the meaning of love, I never let go of John's hand. MS gradually took my husband's ability to walk, to sit upright, to use his arms, and to speak clearly. However, as cruel as the disease was it served as a catalyst to bring out the best in our relationship. It caused me to put my interests on the back burner so I could more fully appreciate the man I married.

Love strengthened John to reach beyond

his limitations. He developed into an outstanding husband and father, a passionate mentor to the disabled, and in the end, the most enthusiastic member of our church.

In our thirty-fifth year of marriage, John developed pneumonia. His immune system was devastated, leaving him unable to fight. As life faded from his face, John gazed at me over the top of a large oxygen mask. His eyes beckoned me near. I nuzzled close and planted a kiss on his cheek, then whispered, "I love you, John."

With a weak smile he mouthed the words, "I love you, too." Then he was gone.

Multiple sclerosis may have won the battle, but love won the war.

— *Laura L. Bradford*

"Love your enemies, do good to those who hate you" (Luke 6:27 NIV), Laura read. How do we show love to someone we're at odds with? The verse tells us implicitly how: "Do good."

When a relationship has faced weeks, months, or even years of being battered by the winds of words, negative emotions, and tough circumstances, lip service is not enough. For one person to believe another's attitude has really changed, the motto becomes "Show me. Prove it."

And consistent good deeds give proof of a change of heart. They show evidence of belief, hope, and trust. They reveal that we care enough to put thought into doing little things. They become irresistible heart-candy.

Do you have a relationship in which you feel as if you're facing an opponent over dueling swords? Want to instill new hope and life and friendship? Then do good deeds.

Lost and Found — Four Sisters

I spent most of my adult life trying to distance myself from my four sisters. Each was wonderful and beautiful, but a painful reminder of a time and place I wanted to forget. In my attempts to erase my childhood, I erased them too, as if they never existed.

I am the youngest of five daughters my mother had in seven years. Mother was a classic beauty in the 1950s, swept away by a handsome man nine years her senior. She married my father when she was just one year out of high school. She once told me she had no bigger dreams than to be a wife and mother. Her childhood home was filled with love from her five rambunctious brothers, parents, and a myriad of aunts, uncles, and cousins who routinely stopped by. She left the only home she knew for one she could not have imagined.

My father was an abusive, raging alcoholic

who did and said things I knew to be evil even if I didn't totally understand. He was a stranger in our lives — staying away for weeks and then reappearing in the middle of the night to wake us all with violence.

I heard none of my father's childhood stories and never saw him as a person. He was a dark silhouette lurking in the doorway of our lives and trapping us in darkness.

We grew up denying he had any effect on us. But he did. Each time we ran half asleep from our beds in our pajamas and watched him beat our mother we were affected — even though I denied it.

Most of the time I played alone or attached myself to neighborhood friends who appeared to have normal families. Whenever my friend had to go inside to eat dinner with her family, I waited outside on the swing set for her return. I often stayed outside long after it grew dark and cold, looking in my friend's windows and feeling something I could not describe.

Eventually my sisters each left for college, marriage, or just to get away from the permanent sadness. My mother spent her days working and caught up in a worried and nervous pace. She had to bear the financial problems my father left during his long absences. When he was back, I spent restless nights worrying if she would leave him and forget to take me.

During my childhood we moved nine times, and with each move the house and situation grew worse. I stayed away as often as I could. When it was finally my turn to leave home, I left for good, with no plans to return.

After college I called home to check on my mother, but I did not stay in touch with my sisters. I had nothing in common with them. I took refuge with friends who didn't remind me of my family. And when holidays came and my friends went to be with their own families, I stayed behind, like I did as a child, waiting for them to return.

Years passed and my mother's situation grew worse. I was living two thousand miles away when my sisters banded together to help my mother start a new life. They freed her from my father. My oldest sister bought her a new house, and the others helped her maintain it by mowing her lawn and bringing her everything from salt for the water softener to groceries.

In time, she was happier than I had ever seen her. I visited her and called her on the phone. I often asked her what I could do for her, and every time she smiled and asked, "Can you stay over another night?"

Years later, when we got the news that she had cancer, I asked her, "Mom, what can I do for you?" She smiled and calmly said, "You can love your sisters. And can you stay over another night?"

As I watched Mom leaving, I felt the same fears I had when I was a child — but this time I was not alone. I had four sisters who each had a part of her inside them. We were so different, yet so much the same. We survived the same childhood and found our own ways out of it toward healthier lives. Most important, we all loved her.

During her illness, I saw how deeply my mother loved each of them. I started to see each of my sisters with her eyes rather than my own. She told me how safe she felt with this one and happy around the other. This one made her laugh and she saw herself in another.

In the days and weeks after her death, I felt such loss. But tucked inside the grief was gratitude to my sisters who each, over the years, gave her something that added greatly to her life: One took her to her doctor's appointments; one answered calls at odd hours; one saw that she never lacked for anything; one gave her a first grandson to love. I love them for what they gave her. My sisters gave her a second chance.

Today we are middle-aged women having the kind of fun we should have had as children but couldn't. I am blessed. I have a wonderful husband and a sweet little boy. I have four sisters whom I love. I no longer sit outside other people's lives and feel alone. I have a family. I even feel my mother's presence when we are together. Through it all I have learned this: Real love is something that is never lost, only sometimes hidden. It merely takes something or someone to help you uncover it — like my sisters.

— Sarah B. Hawkins

As Sarah found, when love plays hide-and-seek, it's not a simple game. When we've allowed love to become hidden, obstructed, or buried, we may not be able to easily bring it back to the surface.

Finding closeness again may take lots of effort. We may have to dig into painful memories. We may have to renew our relationship with others to help us hunt for it. We may have to deal with issues such as forgiveness or understanding others.

But when we uncover hidden love, it's like finding a treasure. We might reap unexpected rewards we could have never imagined! And we might wonder how we ever lived without it.

Some things in life are worth a search — including love, even when it's hiding.

My Knight Knows

"Is your nose crooked?" I asked.

As Richard pondered how to answer my question, I wondered what possessed me to ask something so stupid. This wonderful man was gently pursuing me. If our relationship continued to grow as it had been, my life as a single woman would soon be over. But then I opened my mouth, letting the words tumble out before considering how careless they sounded.

"No . . ." He hesitated. "My nose is perfect. It's the rest of my face that is lopsided." Richard's warm laughter reassured me he could handle my candor.

If you'd asked one of my neighbors about Richard, he would have been identified as the man in button-down shirts and dress pants who arrived at my house in a Toyota Camry. However, I began to believe he was my knight in shining armor. All he lacked was a horse.

Relaxed by his laughter, I took a deep breath, determined to tell him something I feared really would be a deal breaker. "You need to know, Rich, I take antidepressants."

He blinked and waited for more.

"They are one of the medications for my pain management. With antidepressants I can handle it when the pain increases. They give the extra emotional energy I need. Without them I get weepy and kind of fall apart." Feeling slightly ashamed, I bit my bottom lip while I looked down at the floor. Seventy percent of people living with chronic pain are on antidepressants as part of their treatment. Yet at this moment facts didn't matter — only Richard's response seemed important.

He took my hands in his. "Whatever you need to take is okay with me as long as it is under a doctor's supervision. Remember," he looked me in the eye, "I believe love can help heal in ways medical science cannot."

Sweet relief flooded my soul as a smile spread across my face. Several years before this conversation an auto accident had turned my world upside down. Every part of my life was invaded by physical pain. Even as Richard and I talked, my whole body ached, yet I began to believe in his theory. Life felt better with him by my side.

As a single, independent woman in my forties, at times I found it difficult to open up and trust Richard's love. To explain the realities of chronic pain felt even harder. Fifteen years my senior, Richard was wise enough to understand and gentle enough to help me with the process. Before we met he had been happily married, until his wife died of cancer. Through their experience, he knew the relationship a couple shared was more important than physical abilities or limitations. Even though I couldn't pull ropes on his sailboat or join him in a game of racquetball, he was convinced our relationship was worth keeping. A few months later I joyfully agreed, and we were married.

Marrying Richard was an easy decision. It was not as easy to trust him with my pain. Each time the pain increased, I debated when to tell him. Again and again I reminded myself to trust his love through another rough spell. But I still struggled to accept my limitations, so how could I expect him to accept them? I often ended up in tears of frustration, worn out physically and emotionally. No longer the strong, active woman I used to be, insecurities mocked me as I adjusted to my new role as wife. Deep down I wondered if a woman whose body always hurt could really be worthy of a love like Richard's.

Before pain became part of my life I was quite active. In addition to work, three nights a week I was either at dance lessons or a swing dance. Weekends included aerobics on Saturdays and often bicycling for hours after church on Sundays. Vacations regularly included hiking, camping, rock climbing, and even bicycling through Nova Scotia. Although I was basically shy, these activities boosted my confidence and gave me opportunities to meet others.

Then in a split second on a beautiful winter's morning my life was changed. As I sat in my car at a red traffic light and sang with the radio, a truck rear-ended me at full speed. I was left with a rare injury involving permanent nerve and muscle damage to my neck, shoulder, and back. The following year and a half my life revolved around physical therapy, doctors' appointments, and experimental neurosurgery. Unable to work, I lost my job. I no longer had many social outings because so much energy was required to endure the pain. It was a challenging time. Through it all I discovered a deep dependence on God and an inner strength I never knew I had.

At the same time in another corner of my

state, Richard went through his own difficult season of life. Linda, his wife of twenty-three years, lost her battle with breast cancer. As Richard cared for Linda and then endured the grief of her death, he also learned new things about himself and about God. After a few years as a widower, Richard set out to find a new wife with whom to share life. That's when we met.

Hollywood would make us believe that when we fall in love all problems disappear — while beautiful music plays. While Richard brought wonderful new dimensions to my life, my physical pain was a constant.

I remember the first time we canceled plans because I was not up to going out. As a career lieutenant colonel with the air force, Richard was not used to canceling plans of any sort. Though my tears convinced him my pain was real, canceling a dinner date with friends went against his character. As he pondered if my tears were genuine or a form of manipulation, I wondered if he could ever understand how constant pain wore me down and if our marriage would be full of similar disappointments.

In the first weeks of our married life we began a learning process that continues today. We observed the patterns of my energy and pain, figuring out how to best use this information. For example, when we travel I can keep up for three days, but then I need a day of rest, so we plan accordingly. At home I schedule a "daily vacation time" so my body can relax. On our sailboat, we keep special pillows that give my body the comfort and support it needs. And on nights when I can't sleep, Richard has learned to trust that I will be better off if I get out of bed.

After so many years of eating alone, it has been a joy to cook for my husband. But early in our marriage I had to learn to plan ahead for dinner. By the time it was late enough in the day to prepare the meal, I would already be exhausted with little energy left to cook. Too many times it seemed as though I seasoned dinner with my salty tears as I tried to push through the pain.

Since then I have learned to prepare what I can early in the day when I have more energy. Still, on some days I have no energy left to prepare a meal. Instead of crying I tell myself, *Trust Richard's love; let him take care of you.*

Without tears and without drama, I tell him, "I can't do this."

He responds with those three little words

of love: "Let's eat out." We've turned it into a win-win situation. He demonstrates his loving protection for me, I show I trust him to do so, and we are both spared the tears.

We've also developed our own code language. When I am doing well, like a skilled surfer I am "riding the wave" and have a beautiful view of the world. When pain begins to close in, I need only say, "I'm crashing." Richard knows I will soon "wipe out" and asks if he can do anything to help.

In the years since our wedding we have come a long way in trusting each other with my pain. He knows I do not manipulate him by using pain as an excuse. I know I can trust him to support me through increased discomfort.

We have come so far and yet I am still learning. Just last Thursday as we got in the car to meet some friends for a picnic, I felt my imaginary surfboard begin to slip. My energy vanished. My emotions began to tumble. Why I kept quiet, I don't know. I guess I still wanted to be "Wonder Wife."

We were a half mile from home and I reminded myself of Richard's dependable love. I bit my lower lip and said, "I need to tell you, I think I'm crashing."

I felt like a failure. I couldn't keep up with the rest of the world. I looked away from

Richard, forcing away the tears.

He didn't say anything.

At the next opportunity he did a U-turn and began driving home. He reached over, held my hand, and said, "I'm taking you home and putting you to bed so you can rest."

Tears rained down my cheeks. I smiled, so grateful I have learned to trust the protective love of my husband. I thought I heard the sound of horses' hooves against the pavement. I turned to look at Richard just in time to glimpse the sunlight shimmer off his armor. My handsome knight with the crooked nose and wonderful laugh was rescuing me once again.

— *Leslie J. Payne*

How do you spell rescue?

Each of our lives has idiosyncrasies and areas in which we need help. For Leslie, rescue meant her husband's believing her and supporting her in her pain management — even if he didn't fully understand.

Maybe rescue for you means that your spouse takes the children for an outing when they're getting on your nerves. Or maybe rescue means a friend meeting you for dinner when you need to talk. Or helping you with practical responsibilities when you feel overwhelmed.

Thank goodness we don't have to go through the challenges of life alone. We really do need each other. And love often means coming to the rescue when a person we care for needs us.

Today, thank someone for the way he or she rescues you. And be on the lookout for how you can bring relief and rescue to the ones you love.

THE HEARTBEAT OF SPRINGFIELD

Looking through the "I love you" written on the foggy window of my '74 Mustang, I saw figures silhouetted in the bug-shrouded lamplights of the park. Suddenly, they ran toward my car. They were carrying baseball bats. Two strong hits on the right front panel of the car and my date screamed. I covered her head with my arms and pulled her close into my chest.

A face pressed against the foggy glass from outside.

"Hey, there's a girl in this one." They pounded on the glass and said, "Sorry, dude, wrong car."

Then they took off across the park lawn. I rolled down the window, leaned out, and said in my best macho voice, "You guys *better* run!"

"Man, we gotta find a different place to talk," I told my girlfriend as we left the area.

After a long silence she said, "You gotta

get a job — and take me on a real date."

Later, as I dropped her off at her dorm, I thought about how much I liked her. I wondered when I'd know that she really loved me.

The elderly lady had put an ad in the *Springfield News.* I don't remember her name. She was a slender woman and her appearance reminded me of Miss Havisham from that Dickens novel about expectations: the one who was mean and hated men because she was jilted at the altar.

She wore a gray belted cotton dress that had a crisp pleated skirt and a collar that reminded me of one of my grandma's handmade doilies. Her white hair was pulled tighter than seemed possible into a neat bun at the base of her long neck. She had a pointy nose and no lips that I could see. And the only visible wrinkles were on either side of the tight lines of her eyes.

She invited me inside.

"Wait here, young'un," she ordered in a monotone as she glided out of the room. "I've got to see to my husband."

I couldn't imagine her being married.

I bit my lip and stood for what seemed like forever, shuffling my feet as I waited for her return. In the center of the room a table was covered with that same doily-looking material. On the table were cups and saucers: thin, dainty, and fragile, arranged precisely. Nothing out of order.

I stepped back and bumped into a large china cabinet with cut-glass panels. Through the panes I saw delicate little figurines. They were obviously from some far-off place.

"Young'un?"

I jumped. "Yes, ma'am?"

She handed me a box. It was cherrywood with carvings of windmills.

She opened it and took out two white gloves. Putting them on, she said, "You'll work for me." It was a statement of fact, not a question. "And I will pay you — well, I might add — at the end of the day. If you work to my satisfaction, I will have you back another day."

She then took a little silver spoon out of the box, peered at her reflection, and then daintily placed the spoon next to a saucer on the doily-covered table.

"These are for my girls," she said proudly. "We play bridge on Thursdays."

Today was Tuesday.

I followed her outside to the garage. As she pulled out a brand-new push mower she told me how to push the primer button, "exactly three times. And then pull the start cord — just so."

The mower roared to life, and I started down the row. I noticed she had not gone back into the house. She stood there watching me as I went back and forth across her lawn.

When I finished mowing, she had me wipe all the grass off the mower and put it away. Next she told me to sweep the sidewalk, pointing out every blade of grass I had missed.

When I had completed every task to her satisfaction, and as she wrote a check out to me, I asked about her husband.

"He's upstairs," she said. And then: "You will come back next Tuesday, same time."

"Yes, ma'am."

That Friday I took my girlfriend to play racquetball. I thought it would be fun. I took a manly swing at the ball and it sailed toward the front wall of the court. It hit her in the back of the head with a *thunk*. She put her hand to her head and turned to look at me. It wasn't the loving look I'd been striving for.

Tuesday. This week it was mow, then pull weeds in the flower bed. Miss Havisham watched me the whole time through the windows.

■ ■ ■ ■

Our next date was roller-skating with the church group. I held my girlfriend's hand like I'd seen the pros do on TV. Suddenly someone grabbed us from behind. We went down in a heap. My girlfriend landed face-first. Blood was everywhere. She busted her lip and broke a tooth. I hated seeing the blood.

Right then and there, I knew I really, really cared for this girl. But things kept going wrong when we were together. *Does she care for me?* I wondered.

Tuesday again. I mowed the yard and then washed the windows — with vinegar and newspaper!

"It makes them shine better than that bottled stuff," she said without smiling. I wasn't sure if she was joking or not. She stood inside each window as I washed on the outside and pointed to every streak I missed until they were gone. By the time we got to the third side of the house, I'd gotten the hang of it; no more streaks. I was surprised when she left me to my work.

It continued this way week after week, and

my girlfriend kept agreeing to go out with me. We saw each other every day in the library at school, but I wasn't sure that she really loved me.

Over the next couple of weeks Miss Havisham stopped watching me while I worked. It felt good to know she finally trusted me. I noticed she spent a lot of time upstairs. Then one Tuesday I went to get the mower, and she stopped me.

"It's going to rain today. I need your help inside."

Great, I thought. *I'm not good at folding doilies.*

We went upstairs and she took me to a room in the back of the house. Dark wood paneling lined the walls and even the ceiling. In the center of the room stood a bed with no sheets. She took me to a closet and said, "We need to clean this out today."

The closet was filled with clothing — men's suits and shirts, all immaculate.

"He always liked things *just so,*" she said as she folded the clothes and put them in a box marked "Goodwill." I found a stack of old magazines in the back and she quickly said, "Those go in the trash."

Then we started on the shelf above. I was surprised that she was actually helping me with the work. On the shelf were some hats: twenty-three to be exact. I handed a couple to her and she placed them in the box. Next I grabbed an armful and started to hand the bundle to her. They spilled out onto the floor. I thought she might yell at me for being so clumsy.

She reached down and picked one out of the pile. It was a straw hat with a big band of red and blue around it. She held it up and then cocked it sideways.

For the very first time, I saw her smile. Her mouth grew wide. Was that the start of a laugh? She placed the hat on the bed and began to pick up the other hats. She tossed a black bowler and another hat into the trash sack with the magazines. We worked together, sorting out the hats.

Miss Havisham told me how she and her husband had moved to Springfield with the railroad and had started with nothing. She told me that she had been quite the slob when they first got married. I told her I doubted it.

She then picked up a beautiful brown fedora. She dusted it off with her dress, surveyed it for a moment, then reached out and placed it upon my head. Then with a flourishing sweep of her hand, she lowered the brim. I sat in shock. I held my breath. I pushed the brim back up just in time to see a tear fall down her cheek.

She quickly grabbed the hat off of my head and placed it on the bed next to the straw one and said, "I won't need you next week."

My heart sank. "But I need the money to take my girl out."

"You'll make do. I'm sure of it."

We finished packing the boxes and I took them downstairs for her.

"Can I have one of the hats?" I boldly asked.

"I'm taking a vacation for a while," she said, as if she hadn't heard me. "Someone will watch the house for me." She gave me my check.

As I opened the door to leave for the last time, she touched me lightly on the shoulder. As I turned, she placed the straw hat into my hand.

"Here," she said, "see if this one fits you." She looked at me and smiled. The lines next to her eyes wrinkled down to her cheeks.

That week I wore the hat as I took my girlfriend to a place I'd heard about. Under this bridge was a drainage pipe that ran back underneath a road. My friend said the noise was fascinating as the cars drove down the road above the pipe. It would make a *thump-thump* as the cars hit seams along the road above and got louder as they drove toward where you were under the bridge. He said there was a nice place to sit under there, especially with a girl. They called it "The Heartbeat of Springfield."

While we sat there waiting, my girlfriend suddenly looked at me kinda funny, then reached out and tilted my new straw hat to the side and smiled.

I reached up to move it back to the way I'd had it and stopped. I had seen that look before on Miss Havisham's face. Had her husband always moved it to the way he wanted it?

It's strange, I thought. *I only went to work for that lady to get money to keep my girl happy.* I had wondered why Miss Havisham's husband was upstairs all the time and why everything had to be *just so.* Talking to her that last day, I learned she did it all for him. Even cleaning the windows with newspaper and vinegar was his way of doing things, and it was her way of showing him how much she loved him.

In that moment, while looking at my girlfriend, I realized that every date I had taken her on was what I had wanted to do. She always said yes, and even when things went wrong, she never complained. She was willing to do everything my way — just so. It was sad that I never saw Miss Havisham smile until her husband was gone. I wondered if she had enjoyed doing everything "just so," as her husband had wanted it. She had served out of love, but had her husband ever reciprocated? I got the feeling he hadn't.

I felt the hat sitting cockeyed on my head and looked into my girlfriend's smiling eyes. At that instant, there in the Heartbeat of Springfield, I knew deep in my heart that she truly loved me.

But did I truly love her? I knew that I wanted to see that smile every day for the rest of my life.

I tapped the hat, and left it the way she wanted it.

Then in the distance I heard it. As the thumping grew louder my girlfriend sunk her cheek deep into my shoulder. When it was over, I raised her chin, lightly kissed her, and said, "What do you want to do next week?"

A year later we were married — at a place of her choosing.

— *Jon Hopkins*

Loving means serving, as Jon learned from

Miss Havisham. He learned that Miss Havisham's devotion to her husband directed her to try to please him.

But Jon also points out another kind of love he learned — one that takes the time to look at a person we care about and asks, "What does this person want? Am I taking too much control?"

Sometimes we assume that what we want, what we like, is also what the other person likes. But as Jon found, that's not necessarily so. Jon learned to take a long look at his girlfriend and to discover her world, to do the things that would make her smile.

When we learn to look at others' needs and desires and preferences, relationships become win-win situations.

The Girl Who Pierced My Heart

The first day I saw her was in late September on registration day at the university where I was on staff. I volunteered to greet new students, but I avoided this strange arrival.

Her head was shaved except for a forgotten lock of long purple hair hanging in her eyes. The bib overalls were at least three sizes too large and looked like they had been favorites for a long time. Scruffy army boots complemented her outfit.

I had never seen so many piercings on one person, and not one of them had an earring. It was as if she were a human pincushion. Around her neck was a dog collar, which matched the chain that hung from the front pocket of her bibs to her hip pocket.

This was a Christian college. *How on earth does this punker think she is going to represent God looking like that?* I wondered.

I remembered my youngest son had worn long hair and shabby jeans in high school. But now he and his wife are missionaries in Thailand.

I'm sure glad my kids got through that rebellious stage, I thought, never noticing that pride, along with judgment, now hung around my neck tighter than her dog collar.

During the first quarter of school, I ran into this odd girl everywhere I went on campus. She always ate lunch alone, but I made sure I found other staff members to eat with; after all, she was just a student.

One night my husband and I went out for dinner. An unkempt homeless man was on the sidewalk near the restaurant holding out a cup for contributions. I carefully refused to make eye contact as I walked quickly around him.

Something nagged at me during dinner. Hadn't I read somewhere in the Bible that whatever you did to the least of these you were doing it to *me?* (see Matthew 25:40). I could have afforded to drop a dollar or two in that man's cup. Why didn't I?

Later that night I still struggled with the issue of loving the unlovable. Whether it was the homeless man or the punk rocker, I seemed to be judging people by their appearances. How was I expected to befriend

170

someone who didn't smell good or didn't dress as I thought they should?

The outside is a reflection of the inside, isn't it? I justified. Wouldn't others judge me by the company I kept if I hung around with people like that?

It seemed to me the way people dress often says, "Don't talk to me," "Don't touch me," "Don't look at me."

Or could it mean the opposite?

Either way, I wanted to love as God loves — far beyond appearances into the depth of character. I wanted to see through God's eyes.

"Lord, help me love the unlovable," I prayed as I drifted off to sleep.

"Barb," I heard clearly in the middle of the night.

My husband looked like he was asleep, but maybe he was playing games.

"What, Gary?"

"Huh?" he said sleepily.

That's strange, I thought as I drifted back to sleep.

"Barb."

"What, Gary?" I said loudly.

"I didn't call you," Gary answered.

Hm-m-m-m. This sounds like the familiar Bible story of Samuel being called out of his sleep by the Lord. Couldn't be.

Once again I fell asleep, and sure enough there was the voice again.

"Barb."

"Okay, Lord, I'll get up."

I trudged to the living room and waited for God to speak, but nothing came. I turned to the one place I knew He always spoke.

My Bible fell open to 1 John 3:17, "If anyone has material possessions and sees his brother in need but has no pity on him, how can the love of God be in him?" (NIV).

I realized I was being a hypocrite. The unlovable were all around me, but I intentionally ignored them. Everyone has the right to be loved. My love for others needed to be authentic and pure.

The next day the girl in scruffy clothes and purple hair was eating lunch alone as usual.

"May I sit here?" I asked.

"Sure," she responded cheerfully.

"What's your name?"

"Angela."

"I love that name. My husband and I wanted to name our second child Angela, but he turned out to be a boy." Angela and I both laughed easily.

"My name's Barb. Where are you from?"

"Corvallis, Oregon."

"Oh. We lived in Eugene for many years. Now we live in Seattle, but my mom lived in Corvallis."

It was hard to keep from staring at the safety pins hanging from her ears, and I had never seen a piercing between the eyes. *Wouldn't that hurt?*

Angela was easy to talk to, however, so I began eating lunch with her several days a week and greeting her when we passed on campus. Before long I didn't even notice the piercings, purple bangs, or the oversized overalls.

About a month later I noticed a dramatic change.

"Did someone make you take out your piercings?" I asked.

"No," replied Angela nonchalantly. "I just decided to take them out."

She had a pretty little face now that I could see it.

In November, I went to the big chain bookstore in town to do some Christmas shopping. Angela had a table set up outside, wrapping gifts to earn money for a mission trip. I was shopping for a specific journal for my daughter-in-law in Thailand.

Angela and I were buds now. She knew where everything in the store was, so she helped me with my shopping. We had a good time chatting about school and the holidays. This year was going to be very different for her. It would be her first Christmas away from home. Angela was looking forward to making Christmas special for orphans in a needy country.

A few weeks later Angela told me she made so much money wrapping gifts she not only earned enough to pay her way on the mission trip, she made enough to help a couple of the other students with their much-needed mission trip funds.

By Christmas Angela had let her hair grow out, cut the long bangs in front, and dyed that portion to match the rest of her natural light brown hair. Shortly before Angela left for her mission trip, I saw her in a skirt! She looked very cute.

I couldn't stand it. I had to say something.

"Angela, you look darling. What made you change so drastically?"

"Well, I figured if I could look weird and you could love me like that, then I knew I could look normal and other people would accept me, too."

Angela wasn't the only one who changed. When I asked God to teach me to love the unlovable I became more compassionate toward the ones I had judged by their appearances.

I saw who Angela was more than what she looked like. I learned to see through God's eyes. It changed my life, as I now see things with a new heart, a heart to see with His eyes and to love all people.

— *Barbara L. Scott*

In her journey of learning to accept Angela, Barbara wondered if the girl was dressing oddly because she wanted to be left alone . . . or because she was desperately trying to get someone's attention.

Turns out that Angela's appearance was her cry, "Please, someone love me even if I choose to look different." Those who look like they care least about what others think are often the ones who actually care the most what others think of them.

As Barbara learned, we can't be put off by the way a person looks. Looks are no indication of the heart and soul. At most, they might be a way of standing out from the crowd, of saying, "Please notice me. Please befriend me." And sometimes, even, "Please help me."

When we learn to love despite the outward appearance, as Barbara learned, we can find a hidden jewel!

A Wounded Heart
Set Free

Vile, degrading words echoed throughout my neighborhood. Accusations shot off like fireworks, reverberating down the street for all to hear. Who could say such things to her husband, a man everyone knew to be altruistic and loving?

Unfortunately, *I could.* And I did.

I'm not the type to verbally slaughter someone. I'm typically caring and tender. Well, at least I was until I learned of my first husband's infidelity. The truth of his hidden lifestyle pierced my soul. I grieved with every ounce of my being. But as the weeks turned into months, a new emotion penetrated my heart: anger. I had always supported and encouraged him. I had stayed by his side through the good times and the bad. *And my payback is this?*

The graphic details of his sexual addiction further incensed me. Raw emotions boiled inside as friends and family took his side.

How? Why? This isn't my fault! Why aren't they supporting me? My indignation kept mounting. I burst in a way that made a volcano look tame. Rage poured out of me.

Nearly a year later, my anger had somehow subsided. Some friends introduced me to A.J., an extremely kind man. We talked casually at a small get-together. A month later, he asked me if I'd go on a date with him.

Fear consumed me despite the good qualities I detected in him. I had once known love and it had cost me everything. I had nothing left to give, while fearfully protecting the few remaining portions of my spirit that weren't scarred. I tried pushing him away, but he was gently persistent. I finally accepted the date. We began seeing each other regularly, and regardless of my apprehension I soon found myself falling in love.

A.J. met me at Chuck-E-Cheese's Pizza one night for my daughter's birthday party. After playing games, opening presents, and eating cake, we took Samantha to her dad's house and then drove back to the restaurant to get A.J.'s truck. As we sat in that most unlikely place, our conversation turned to an even more unlikely subject: marriage.

I loved A.J. as fully as my wounded heart

allowed, but I knew I couldn't enter a covenant relationship with him until I recovered more from the pain of my first relationship. He graciously agreed to wait as long as I needed. I couldn't offer any time-line; I just rested in the fact that I'd know when it was time.

That day came several months later. Filled with quiet confidence, I looked into the eyes of the one who had so patiently overcome my fear of love and said, "I'm ready."

A.J.'s face shone. As fluffy snowflakes swirled around me and the pine trees faded into the background I heard a familiar voice ask, "Amy, will you marry me?"

My head stopped spinning as I realized I still hadn't answered and A.J. was about to ask me a third time. "Yes!" I cried out with all of my being.

Four months later, my name changed. I was no longer Amy Jenkins, but Amy Cha-nan. I was also no longer the considerate, caring person A.J. had grown to adore. My mind only knew of one way to be a wife. I unwittingly replicated the same poor habits my first husband and I had created. My heart knew that married life did not have to mean constant fighting, but my mouth kept going into autopilot, spewing harmful words at the man I most cherished.

I hated myself for the way I treated A.J. I had a second chance at love and was married to an incredible man, but I knew I would destroy our relationship if I didn't change. I tried with all my might, but voices from the past haunted me. I remembered the numerous times my first husband told me of my anger problem. I pondered my family's words during my angry phase of grief. "Amy, we've never seen this side of you before." "You shouldn't let this upset you so much." "Amy, we're all scared of you." *I guess I really am an angry person,* I finally told myself.

I hated that fact. I taught Bible studies and did community service. I lived a good life, except for my one not-so-secret secret: My temper continued to escalate. I was cordial to strangers, but those closest to me saw a different side, a facet that hurt them and devastated me.

I didn't want to be mad. I simply didn't know what else to do.

During yet another round of anger, I decimated A.J. with demeaning words. I don't even remember why I was upset or what I yelled, but I clearly recall the raw rage and heightened emotion I felt. I was ready for that reckless game of escalation my "ex" and I played for so long. But instead of engaging me, A.J. did the unthinkable.

He gently placed his hands squarely on my shoulders, looked me straight in the eye, and said, "Amy, I know this isn't you. You've been hurt and what you're doing is just a reaction to that."

The self-imposed shackles that bound me for so long fell to the floor as tears streamed down my face.

"I'm sorry. I'm so very sorry" was all I could manage to say between sobs. "Please forgive me."

A transformation occurred in me that evening. I won't say I never exploded again or that I suddenly figured out what it meant to love *and* be married. Those came with time. But in that most sacred of moments, A.J. gave me a priceless gift by looking beyond my behavior and into my bleeding heart. He freed me from needing to live out the label I shamefully bore. He repeatedly pointed out my attributes and prevented me from focusing solely on my shortcomings. And he taught me to love others *and* myself.

People ask me how I could possibly love again after everything I went through in my first marriage. My answer is simple: "You'd have to know A.J. He made it easy to love."

— *Amy Chanan*

Hurt people hurt other people. The saying is often true. Like a wounded animal, when a person lives in a world of pain, her personality often becomes skewed. She may lash out in anger at those nearest.

When we are hurt, it often takes us longer than we expect to recover from the pain and trauma. Sometimes, the least sign of stress or reminder of the painful situation can bring all the emotions rushing back — even though we may not be consciously aware of the connection at that moment. As Amy experienced, we may find ourselves blowing up with anger, fear, or other emotions we experienced in painful situations.

So what do we do when someone we love still has dregs of emotional issues from the past? Perhaps the first thing to do is to remember the pain the person has gone through. That helps us keep from taking angry or harsh words personally. At another time, after the emotion has subsided, we can non-threateningly ask, "Are you feeling like you're in the same situation you were in before? What can we do about this?"

When we truly love, we look at the source of the pain. And though we don't accept abuse, love looks beyond the painful past of the person we love, and into a hopeful future.

ENTERING MOLLY'S WORLD

"Okay!" I brightly told my Brownies at our first meeting. "Now hold up your right hand and stick up these two fingers, like this. Other hand, Denise. No, two fingers, please, Molly. Molly?"

Molly just stared at me through her thick glasses. Her eyes were slightly crossed.

"Molly, two fingers, like this. See, you can use your thumb to cover the other —"

"*No!* Don't touch me!"

I jerked my hand back, startled. Molly's hand was now a fist.

Okay, I thought, *we'll just let this issue drop.*

"Good job, girls! Now let's say the Brownie Promise together, shall we?"

I had become a Brownie Girl Scout as a second grader. My mother, who had been a Scout as a girl, was our leader. She and I stuck with scouting until I went to college, and even then she kept our Mariner Girl Scout troop several more years. Scouting was definitely in my blood.

I led a Brownie troop in college and decided this was the age group for me. Smiling little faces under brown beanies, eager eyes looking up at me for guidance . . . what more could a woman ask?

So when I moved to Colorado and found myself alone, too depressed to hold a job, desperately in need of distraction and something to do, I started a Brownie troop.

One day a few weeks later, we were sitting in a circle, cutting out paper shapes for a collage. Nothing was particularly attractive about the tiled meeting room at the trailer park where we met, but those nineteen little faces, concentrating on their work, made a lovely sight.

"Is this a good picture for 'kind to animals,' Mrs. Dodge?"

"That's a great one, Stephanie!"

"Here's people hugging. Can it go with 'friend to all'?" Karen asked.

Suddenly Molly jumped up, ran across the circle, and tried to stab Karen. Luckily, we were using blunt plastic scissors.

"Molly!" I said when I had rescued Karen, calmed the other children, and taken Molly aside to talk. "What was that about?"

Molly looked up at me, her black eyes unfocused. Her Brownie beanie was surrounded by uneven clumps of hair poking out in different directions. Molly's hair looked as if she had cut it herself with dull scissors, which, I discovered later, she hadn't. But she was so afraid of being hurt, so sure that the hairdresser was planning to kill her, that her mother could only trim her hair on the run: snip a bit off on this side, wait for her to calm down, walk by and snip the other side.

"I had to hurt her back!" Molly told me. "I had to stop her!"

"But, sweetie, what did Karen do to you? She was just sitting there, on the other side of the room!"

"She was thinking lies about me!"

I put an arm around her shoulders.

"Moll, she wasn't thinking lies about you. We don't know what other people are thinking."

"I heard her! She was thinking lies! And I had to stop her! I *had to!*"

At home that evening, I tried to think the situation through. Molly was one of three girls in the troop who were developmentally delayed. But this seemed bigger than her having trouble comprehending, and I wasn't sure I wanted anything to do with it. After all, I was looking for responsive little girls whom I could gently guide into responsible womanhood. Molly, on the other hand, was just plain *odd.*

"Can you tell me a little about Molly?" Seeking some answers, I visited her special needs classroom and talked with her teacher.

"She's crazy!" Mrs. Blixen answered. "I can't teach her at all!"

I volunteered in the classroom, learned a great deal about developmental delays, and discovered even more about how different this child was, even from her disabled classmates.

One day we were working on letter books. Each day we learned a new letter, then cut out pictures that started with that letter and pasted them in the books. Mrs. Blixen had catalogs from Sears and Wards for the children to cut up as necessary.

We had started with A — apples, alligators, and angels from Christmas cards.

"Ants! Stamp on the ants!" Molly yelled as she ran around the room stomping on invisible bugs.

Then on to B — boys, bicycles, bananas from newspaper food ads.

"No! No! Too loud! Too loud when the balloon pops!"

And Molly hid under the teacher's desk, hands over her ears, whimpering, oblivious to the fact that the only balloon around was on paper.

"This is the story of the little red hen," Mrs. Blixen read at storytime one afternoon.

Very quietly, eyes on her teacher, Molly started sliding her chair forward, inch by inch. As she approached, she started swinging her foot. The foot moved closer to Mrs. Blixen with each swing.

From her expression and movements, it was clear she was planning to kick her teacher when she got close enough.

Before she did it, though, she suddenly jumped up and started to cry.

"Stop it!" she screamed. "Stop it! Don't you kick me!"

Was she playing the scene in her head — sliding her chair up and kicking the teacher's leg; the teacher is angry and kicks back; Molly protests? I didn't know.

I had a degree in elementary education, but no one had ever described a child like Molly. I could see little point in trying to teach her; we had enough trouble just containing her. But somehow I couldn't walk away from that troubled little spirit. She wasn't clever, and she certainly wasn't attractive, yet for some reason she had wound her way into my heart.

When I started working with Molly, handicapped children were in their own self-contained classes, carefully labeled by their disability. A child with more than one handicap was often unplaceable, as she wouldn't "fit" in either class.

Molly's behaviors were too disturbed for the class of developmentally delayed children, and her functioning was too low for the disturbed class. If she couldn't be placed in any classroom, she qualified for homebound instruction. This involved the district hiring a teacher to teach her for a few hours each day.

Someone in the school system hired me to be her homebound teacher and placed us both in the class for disturbed children. As long as I would work with Molly's low academic level, the teacher of that class was willing to address her behaviors.

In Molly's class I discovered I had a gift for reaching disturbed children. I found I had compassion for, and insight into, the divergent thought processes of my students.

For example, Molly could not learn to add. But, oddly enough, she could subtract.

"If you have two apples, and someone gives you another one, how many apples do you have?"

"I dunno! I don't like apples anyway, so who cares?!" Molly giggled and started to leave her desk.

"Wait a minute, Moll. If you have three books, and you lose one, how many do you have left?"

"Two! You're mean to take my book! Give it back!"

We finally figured out that she related to losing things, or having things taken away, but couldn't believe anyone would give her more of something.

Despite the shattering effect of a divorce on my already shaky self-esteem, I managed to register for a degree program to teach educationally handicapped learners. I wasn't doing enough for my Molly. I wanted to learn more. As I studied, I tried to connect everything I learned with this special little girl.

"Now, if you were going to the store to buy bread for your mother, and you lost the money, what would you do?"

This is part of a test of common sense and judgment. Molly didn't get credit for it, although she apparently did understand the main issue.

She jumped up, raised her fist, and yelled at the surprised tester, "Don't you steal my money!"

Master's degree finally in hand, I was hired to teach emotionally and behaviorally

189

disordered children in a local school district. I hadn't been able to teach Molly for years, but I couldn't turn my back on her. I stayed in touch with her and her parents, tracking her in and out of special classes, residential programs, and mental hospitals.

I have now taught special needs children for more than three decades. And I've had some notable successes, as the world would gauge them, such as a developmentally delayed girl who successfully used sign language as a bridge to reading.

And I've had my failures, of course, such as one young man who is currently serving a life sentence for murder. I hope he remembers, in the darkest hours of the night, that way back in fourth and fifth grade, Mrs. Dodge loved him.

Because for me, that's the key. I love these kids, every one of them — bright or confused, mean or sweet, manipulative or compliant, grateful or antagonistic, married with a family or registered sex offender. They're mine, part of my heart, forever. And I'll do anything I can to help them.

Molly died of congestive heart failure when she was twenty-two. Her mother phoned me after the service, crying.

"I don't understand why God even let her be born!" she said. "Molly was never really happy. She wasn't any good to anyone, and nothing was any good for her. Her life was useless and miserable! How could God let her live that way for all those years?"

"I don't mean to try to speak for God," I offered. "But I do know this. Because of Molly, I got my degree in special education. And I've helped a lot of children over the years. I wouldn't have worked with any of those children if I hadn't known Molly. So as far as I'm concerned, she gets credit for every child I've been able to help have a better life."

I don't know if that made any difference to Molly's mom or not. It changed my perspective, though. I realized that Molly had helped me immensely. Because of Molly, I discovered a gift for working with special learners, got my master's degree, and found my lifelong career. My love for her, her involvement in my life over more than a decade, had a transforming power. And the life transformed by that love was mine.

— *Elsi Dodge*

When Elsi discovered that Molly was different than other children, she noted that she would have rather not been bothered. And she probably could have arranged that — she could have told Molly's parents that the girl couldn't come to Brownies.

But Elsi chose differently. Instead of withdrawing, she decided to draw closer to Molly. She chose to show affection to a little girl who probably didn't get much kindness.

The more warmth Elsi expressed, the more she cared for Molly and wanted to do what was necessary to help her. Sometimes love is like that . . . the more we give, the more we learn to love, and the more we want to show that love.

And that's the kind of love that changes lives! When we give, we receive.

JUST CALL ME BABE

My mouth said, "I do." My brain yelled, *What are you doing here?*

In a sense, this all seemed so sudden. And wasn't I too old to be getting married? But as I looked into Pete's eyes, I knew that, yes, this was what I wanted — what I wanted with all my heart!

The preacher said, "I now pronounce you . . ."

Before he could finish, Pete grabbed me, planting on me a brand-new-husband's kiss. He turned to his son, the best man, triumphantly raising his fist, a wild smile slashing his cheeks, his blue eyes dancing with tears.

Grasping my hand, he said, "Come on, Babe. Let's eat our cake and get out of here."

Babe! He called me BABE! No one had ever called me Babe before!

I watched him, mouth full of wedding cake, pounding backs, shaking hands, looking at his watch, motioning me to *get with it . . . let's go!*

Later in the car, on our way to our wedding night, my mind went in the wrong direction. Widowed two years after having been married to a good man for thirty years, I was now married to that good man's best friend. Pete had lost his wife shortly after my Bill had died, and in comforting each other, we had found our way down the aisle.

Bill had been the perfect father and was a good husband, but was a workaholic, so we had little time for romance. Our "extra" time was spent involved in the children's activities. In all those years, his name for me had been *Mama*.

And why not? I had birthed four babies within five years. After that we seldom had much private time. Ironically, according to Pete, his marriage to Jayne followed the same pattern. So here we were — a forty-nine-year-old mama of four grown children and a sixty-three-year-old daddy of two grown-ups, headed for a night of motel madness.

When we arrived at the motel, Pete unlocked the door, followed me in, slammed the door, locked it, and dropped our suitcases to the floor. He slipped out of his jacket, yanked off his tie with one hand, and unbuttoned his shirt with the other. My mind was a blank. I wanted to go home and hide in a closet. Bill was the only man I'd ever been with, and our intimate times had been few and far between after the children were born — and always under the cover of darkness.

"Okay, Babe," Pete said, his eyes aglow behind his dark-rimmed glasses.

Giggling like a teenager, I pulled my blouse from my skirt and seventeen years of magical marriage began.

Not long after that we were visiting my sister and her husband. I heard Pete call her *Babe.* My heart constricted.

Later in bed, Pete began to snore. I leaned over his shoulder. "Pete," I said. He snored on.

I tried again.

"Rumph . . . mph . . . mmmm. . . ."

"Pete, don't you ever call anyone else *Babe*," I said. "That's *my* name."

Mr. Romantic didn't answer, but he'd stopped snoring.

I waited a second and then plopped my head on my pillow, pulled up the covers, and waited for sleep to come.

Over the years, every morning welcomed a dream-come-true day. I found that romance doesn't have to be a dozen roses and dinner by candlelight at a posh restaurant. Romance doesn't have to be expensive. Romance isn't something that takes mountains of effort; it just takes caring and a little creativity — like Wife's Day.

My first Wife's Day came that fall when we went to the Oklahoma State Fair. On the way, Pete said, "Now, we're not going to spend any money. We're just going to look."

At the end of the day, back in the car, headed for home, Pete pitched a sack packed in red tissue paper onto my lap. He grinned like a circus clown, his blue eyes squinched in laughter, his white hair curling above his ears and over the lower edge of his blue denim cap.

"I thought you said we couldn't spend any money."

"*We* didn't. *I* did. It's for Wife's Day. Open it!"

He watched me pull out a brown and red leather billfold and read the little white card, covered with his scribble and tied to the handle of the sack: "Love ya, Babe."

Before I could cry, he said, "That's in case you ever have money to spend, you'll have something to carry it in."

After that, we celebrated Wife's Day so many times and in so many ways: special invitations to supper, shopping trips for clothes I didn't need, craft shows, sight-seeing ventures across states, breakfast in bed. . . .

I lost count of the times I answered the doorbell to find a lady from the flower shop holding a crystal vase with a long-stemmed red rose, a white card in her hand, biting her lips to keep from laughing. "Is this where Babe lives?" or "Is Babe home?" or "Can you tell me where to find Babe?"

After he retired, Pete would come by the school where I taught and leave notes on my car. Once a student named Sean came into the classroom waving a scrap of paper.

"Hey, y'all!" he yelled. "Look what I found." He turned to me and said, "Mrs. Smith, who's Babe? This says, 'Meet me at Fred's Fish House. Love ya, Babe.' "

The class erupted into laughter.

I reached for the paper. Sean held it over his head. "Why, Mrs. Smith, are *you* Babe?"

After that, he'd yell when leaving the classroom or when he'd see me in the hall, "See ya, Miss Babe."

Another time, Gary needed to borrow a pencil. I told him to get one from my desk drawer.

A moment later I heard him laugh. He held up a pencil for all to see: "Mrs. Smith? Who's Darlin'?"

I grabbed at the pencil, my face burning. Gary held it out of reach. "Hey, all, listen to what's carved in the pencil: 'Hello, Darlin'.' "

Pete had come to school a few days before and had waited in my room while I attended a brief faculty meeting. While there, he'd spent his time being creative.

After those two incidents, my students looked for more messages left by Mr. Romantic. Though I tried to find them first, many times they beat me to the punch.

We found inscriptions worked in among the notes in my plan book: "Love ya, Babe"; printed in tiny letters on the board under lines of daily assignments: "Hello, Darlin' "; printed on pages of my desk calendar: "Pete loves Donna."

Those mutual searches created camaraderie between my students and me. Still today, when I see a student somewhere in public, I get a wave and a "Hi, Miss Babe!"

Even after all they discovered, though, I didn't tell them of Mr. Romantic's way of expressing love in public, our secret hand squeeze — three for "I love you" and four for "I love you, too."

Nor did I tell them that he filled my car with gas so I didn't have to get out in the heat or the cold. Or that he sent me romantic cards for every occasion, even for those he invented: Wife's Day, Lover's Day, Best Mate's Day. . . .

The last year of Pete's life, he struggled with lung cancer and congestive heart failure. Because he wanted to be where he could see me every minute, we set up a hospital bed in the living area of our home. No matter what I needed to do or wanted to do for him, his response was "Get on that computer, Babe. Write a story so I can brag that I married an author."

One day as I pecked away, thinking he was asleep, suddenly Pete said, "Hey, Babe, you know what? I have your picture in my heart."

My heart took over my whole body and my throat constricted. I went to his bedside and held him close. I told him I loved him more than anything in the world. I kissed him and told him he was my whole life.

"Love ya, Babe." He patted my cheek, traced his finger along my lips. "Now get back on that computer."

I laughed, went back and sat down, and just as I poised to peck, I heard a horrible sound. Pete's body was drawn into a twisted shape, his head jerking.

For the next four weeks, I sat with him day and night in a nursing center, under hospice care. Though he never spoke again, once when I held his hand, his fingers pressed mine three times.

Two years after he died, I finally had the courage to open the scrapbook of our wedding pictures. I found a yellow sticky note pressed on the inside cover: "Love ya, Babe."

Pressing that note to my lips, I knew the magical seventeen years of perfect love would be with me forever.

Today, eight years later, Mr. Romantic continues to whisper in my ear: "Hello, Darlin' "; "Love ya, Babe." Yes, I'll always be my sweetheart's *Babe.*

— *Donna Smith*

"How do I love thee? Let me count the ways. . . ." Elizabeth Barrett Browning wrote . . . and Pete Smith lived! Good, steady love is a blessing, a solid core in our lives. But when you top that solid core with romance, well, it's like icing on the cake. Cake can get pretty dry and be pretty basic. But a bit of icing takes it from good to great and enhances the experience.

Adding romance to the solid core of your love takes time. It also requires creativity — or a good Google search, so none of us really has the excuse that we're just not creative.

Want to enhance your relationship and sweeten your marriage experience? Add a little icing to the cake. Find the fun little ways to say, "I love you, and I like you, too!"

When Sara Taught
Me Freedom

While I was blessed as a child to have been loved by many, my grandmother Sara loved me differently. Most relationships in my life fit neatly within a set of laws I had either created or accepted — no questions asked. The rules were easy to follow and made perfect sense: If people loved me, I was lovable. If I pleased people, I was happy. If I displeased them, then they were right to be disappointed.

But this was not Sara's love. I knew Sara loved me because she often told me so, because she demonstrated it every time we had fun together, and because when I messed up, she still adored me. With Sara, I was accepted without expectation or exception, so I had no need to please or to perform. I was simply a delight to her, and it felt like freedom. It was easy to love Sara back.

But as I got older, I had a harder time

believing all the wonderful things about myself that Sara would say. Maybe I became too busy to spend enough time with Sara, and her voice dimmed in comparison to what others told me. Maybe I was actually more comfortable out in the world because my system was working; I was striving and people were noticing me. Maybe I was ashamed of some of my mistakes. Whatever the reason, when Sara gushed, I deflected her blessings and resisted her praises because I felt they could not be true.

Thankfully her love eventually proved more powerful than my ability to resist it. Even as her mind wasted away with Alzheimer's disease, Sara's affection would never end, which was very good because I needed it more than ever after my child was born.

When our first child arrived I named her Sara after her great-grandmother. I had visions of her twirling in monogrammed dresses with bows in her hair. Of course she would be the first of her peers to talk and walk, and she would delight her preschool teacher because she was so precious and precocious. My daughter Sara would have impeccable manners, grooming, and wardrobe. She would be sweet to younger children yet able to carry on a conversation with any adult in any setting. She would undoubtedly be a straight-A student, president of her class, homecoming queen, winner of the talent show, and a great athlete with a dainty frame. And I would, of course, love every minute of it.

When my daughter Sara turned out to be a child who didn't care what people thought about her, what she looked like, or how she presented herself, I was baffled. For a person who looked just like me, she couldn't have been more different. Actually, when I wasn't exasperated with her, I secretly envied her. I had not experienced the freedom she exhibited since I was a child with my grandmother, yet I fought her freedom with a vengeance. Under the guise of helping Sara be more acceptable to others and appreciated by them, I forced her to comply with my expectations. In reality, I was trying to make her more acceptable and appreciated by *me.*

Whenever I would make her look the part of a perfect daughter, like making her wear pretty dresses and bows, she would balk, and I would shout and shame her. It definitely wasn't the motherhood I had expected, and it left me feeling that I had failed as a parent. Truthfully, what I had failed to do was to love Sara for the person that God had created her to be and not for the person I thought she should be.

"Why can't you just let me be me?" Sara would plead in desperate frustration.

Sometimes I felt like I didn't like her, and it scared me. Somewhere along the way, I had lost sight of the fact that my deepest desires for my daughter had been fulfilled all along: She was healthy and had a sweet spirit that I had wanted for her more than anything when she was an infant. But as she got older, I expected more from her. Now we were both tethered to my weighty expectations, and they were drowning her, too. As her parent, I needed to cut us both free.

During these years my grandmother Sara's mind was deteriorating quickly. I actually thought I was praying in love when I prayed she would die. After all, she had lived a full life with no regrets and we knew she was going to heaven; surely there was no purpose left for her on this earth, trapped in the Alzheimer's wing of her nursing home.

When I visited Sara, she and I might sit in silence for an eternity, but then she would start talking. Typical of conversations with people who have dementia, Sara and I would talk about the same things over and over. Sara seemed to no longer remember who I was or anything about me, so I wondered if God was really talking to me through her familiar words: "I love you. I'm so proud of you," she would say. "You are so beautiful." "You're doing such a good job." "The good Lord sees you and knows that you are a good mother."

Then the greater miracle happened: I actually began to believe those things about myself again. And that's when I started believing them about my daughter, too.

The complete irony of my withholding love from my daughter for not being more like me was that I did not even like myself, especially as a mother. All my life I had loved other people *if* they proved lovable. But Sara lived free from expectations. In fact, both Saras lived free from them, and I could no longer resist either one of them.

For what was perhaps the first time in my life, I would love first and love fiercely, like my grandmother. Coaxing performance from my daughter so I could love her back was not love at all; it was control, and I would have no more of it.

One October morning when Sara was in first grade, I resolved to release her from the chains of expectation I had placed around her. I wanted to consciously set her free to become the person she was created to be. Whatever it took, whatever it looked liked, whatever she looked like, I would not fight it anymore.

My track record since that fall morning many years ago has not been perfect, but I can say that since then I have truly loved my daughter. And I like her. She is so lovable and likeable, not because I made her that way but because she was born that way.

Finally I understood that the familiar words of my grandmother also fit my daughter: "I love you." "I'm so proud of you." "You are so beautiful." "You're doing such a good job." "You will make a great mother someday."

When I started saying these words to my daughter and meant them, they were like a lifeboat for us. I could say I am forever indebted to my grandmother for loving me so faithfully and freely my whole life, in spite of myself, until I believed it. I could say that I owe my daughter for setting me free from the superficial law of reciprocation that I had tried to pass off as love. But according to the love that they taught me, I don't owe them a thing.

— *Nancy Page Sheek*

Love is purest when it's unfettered by chains of expectations. The wisest man who ever lived, Jesus, told His followers, "Give as freely as you have received!" (Matthew 10:8).

This also applies to our relationships with others. We are each created individually and uniquely. We each have a purpose in the overall scheme of life and eternity. And our personalities — the way we were made — play an intricate part in fulfilling our roles in life. Others who love us accept us and appreciate us — personality quirks and all.

As we consider others, we remember that they are created with a purpose. That they are unique. That they are not designed to be our personality twins or our alter egos or other versions of ourselves. Instead, their own form has a function. To love others means to free them from our unreasonable expectations that they should be or think a certain way.

Just as we've experienced affection freely given from others, we can free others with our unfettered love.

The Good With the Bad

"Tell me something about him that you like."

"I like how he makes me laugh, how good he is with kids, how friendly he is, how kindhearted —"

"Tell me something about her that you like."

"I like that she's loyal. . . ."

That's how our marriage counseling session started: my naming a hundred good things about him and his answering with a thing or two about me. Our pastor would ask one of us a question and then ask the same question of the other.

Like so many couples today, our relationship was not the traditional: meet, date, fall in love, get married, have kids. Shortly after we started dating, I was with child. With a communication breakdown, we broke up at the beginning of the pregnancy.

Single, alone, and with a baby, my mind-set changed to focus on the little life that was now my responsibility. I wanted to have my son baptized — not because I understood the meaning, but because family members insisted it was the right thing to do. I didn't go to church because I never felt comfortable and couldn't relate to the preaching. But then I found a church that was like home and a pastor who preached in a language I understood.

Within months my son's father got back in touch with me and we worked things out.

Before long baby number two was on the way. By the time our daughter was a year old, we had settled in our relationship, started going to church together, and established a personal relationship with our Lord Jesus. Everything was going great. We had two children, a relationship with God, a church family, and a pastor whom we could relate to on a personal level. That's when Marvin proposed.

I was like a dog wagging his tail when he sees his owner. My eyes saw nothing but sunshine. Heaven visited earth and placed a tall, handsome man in my life, and he was about to become my husband. If being in love blinds a person, getting engaged made me blind, deaf, and — okay, dumb. Not because I was getting married or because of whom I was marrying, but I only saw what I wanted to see: a perfect world of love!

Even with the past problems that had led to our breakup, at that point I only knew we were perfectly in love, with no troubles or faults.

So you can imagine how surprised I was that we had to take a counseling class. After all, we had two children together and were in love. I thought we'd set the date and the rest would be happily ever after.

When my pastor mentioned the marriage counseling, I thought, *Okay, so the pastor will just counsel us — wait, we don't need counseling. We're getting married.*

Then I decided, *No problem — get the marriage counseling out of the way and move forward to the wedding.*

My pastor is a pretty clever guy. I think he was looking to see if the relationship was real. No one would believe it was a real relationship the way I floated into the office.

"Tell me something about him you don't like," the pastor said.

"Umm, let me see, I, uh — uh, well, I can honestly say there is more about him that I like than I don't like."

"Okay, so name something you don't

like." My pastor was not about to let me off easy.

I searched my brain for something about my husband-to-be that I didn't like. I thought of making up something just to get out from under the interrogation light. But I came up blank.

"I honestly can't think of anything I don't like about him," I answered with the corners of my lips touching my ears and all my teeth gleaming.

When the pastor asked Marvin the same question, not even a half second passed before he started naming things.

"I don't like the way she _____ or the way she _____ and the way she or the _____."

I could not believe he would say those things to our pastor. I defended all the things he named. Each time I spoke, my voice gained more depth and the corner of my mouth slowly receded from my ears to my chin. Finally, fuming, my arms crossed, my eyebrows crunched together, and my vision returned. He didn't have wings; he wasn't perfect.

"What about your _____ and your _____ and _____," I countered.

I went into the session as a newly engaged woman with the joy of a tail-wagging dog, but turned into a teeth-clenching, mouth-foaming, growling attack dog.

Then my pastor did the oddest thing. He closed his book and said, "Okay, you have my blessing to get married."

What? I thought.

I was annoyed with the entire male race. How could we have his blessing when we were about to reach hurricane-force winds strong enough to blow open his office? And how could the love of my life find so many things wrong with me when I hadn't mentioned one thing about him? And worse, how could he name them in front of the pastor?

I wish I could remember the day when I realized I was the only one in that room with blinders on. I was blind, deaf, and dumb to everything because I was so in love with the idea of marrying the man of my dreams. But the other two people in that counseling session realized that real relationships have real ups and downs. My grandmother would say, "Take the good with the bad."

I think my pastor wanted to make sure we didn't just feel obligated to marry because we had children. I think Marvin, also a clever guy, figured out what the pastor was doing and began answering honestly. It was a wake-up call to bring the dreamy nuptials up front and personal.

Relationships are not the perfect picture I was painting for myself. Matrimony does not mean you get the person of your dreams, buy a house, have kids that excel socially, physically, intellectually, and eventually are financially topped with a happily ever after.

In the past seventeen years I've spent with my husband, I've realized that real, bona fide relationships are successful as two people struggle to overcome their differences for the good of each other.

My grandmother would say, "As surely as you live, you will see trouble some days." When a relationship is built on false pretenses or exaggerated expectations, and trouble arrives, the relationship has no foundation to stand on. Then the troubled relationship becomes like a house built on sand, and when the strong forces come, the house goes down.

Relationships that survive are the sum of love, trust, values, faithfulness, and commitment, but the glue to hold it all together is the ability to quickly forgive each other. In order to forgive, each must be able to admit and accept a wrong. The relationship will flourish when both parties can recognize that they will face hills and valleys before they reach the mountaintop.

As my grandmother would say, "In life, you'll have some good days and some bad days; so you might as well take the good with the bad."

— *Sheila Farmer*

As long as we live on earth, none of us humans will be perfect. And it doesn't take very long for that reality to become evident in relationships.

Sometimes we enjoy our bond with another so much that we only see how great the person is and focus on how much we enjoy that connection. At times it's easy to forget that another person is human. So when that humanity suddenly rears its head, we can feel surprised and disillusioned and disappointed.

That's when we need to remember the wise concept Sheila learned: In relationships, as in life in general, we'll face good times and bad times. Every person has positive traits and negative traits, no matter how seldom we notice the negatives. Love doesn't mean wearing blinders — it means honestly taking the good with the bad.

Everyday Adventures With Mom

"Reverend Waters, you've gotta come to the church and get your mom!"

I listened in shock as the woman on the line told me that my mother had gone to the front of the church, grabbed the microphone, and proceeded to curse at everyone.

My mom? Surely not! That wasn't like her at all!

When I arrived at the church, she was sitting in the choir room like nothing had happened.

"Why are you here?" she asked me. She had no memory of her actions.

As I led Mom away I was deeply concerned.

Being the youngest of three children, I have always had a special bond with my mother. She spoiled me because I am her "baby." She has loved me unconditionally.

As a child and teen I depended on her for everything. But after my father died thirty years ago, she started to grow more dependent on me. My two older sisters got married and moved out of state, but I attended a local college; I did not want to leave my mother all alone.

I loved talking with my mother about so many things, like my latest romantic interest. She often gave me insight that could only come from a wise mother. We went shopping together and spent hours laughing as we tried on big ugly hats and fancy dresses just for fun. We often went to the movies and laughed until we cried. And on our outings, we often ended up at the grocery store, buying vanilla ice cream to share after dinner.

About fifteen years after my father died, I decided to attend seminary in another state. Mom flew to my graduation even though she'd just had knee reconstruction surgery and the doctor had told her to stay home. Her love for me overruled the doctor's orders.

After graduation, I returned home, caring for Mom while she recuperated from the surgery. When she could walk again, I got a full-time ministry position in a town not too far from where Mom lived and moved into my own home.

Over time, Mom started having physical

problems. She kept losing her balance and falling. Her equilibrium was awry. The doctors put her on medicine and gave her a cane. Mom did not like being seen with a cane.

"I'm not crippled. I'm fine," she would announce as she grabbed my arm for support.

Then she started to forget things. I would ask about her doctor's appointment, and she would say, "Oh, I forgot all about it."

Now this latest experience was just one more indication that something was wrong. My sisters and I decided to make an appointment for Mom with a neurologist at the earliest possible date, which was two months away.

One morning my oldest sister called me in a panic. Around midnight the night before, her friend had been driving the main highway where Mom lives. He saw my mom walking down the street in her nightgown and slippers. He was afraid to blow the horn because he didn't want to startle her. My sister wanted to know what to do.

I drove over to my mom's house and talked with her. I calmly asked her about going out the night before. She denied it. However, she did admit finding herself on the front porch with her nightgown on and not remembering how she got there.

I recognized that my mother's medical problems were more serious than I first thought. I started spending the night with her to keep her safe. After many tests, the doctors determined that Mom had had a silent stroke, which caused her to have seizures. During the seizures, Mom would lose all inhibitions and have no knowledge of the present.

The doctor put her on medication to control her seizures. Mom did fine when she took the medication. However, she'd often say, "I don't need that stuff. I feel fine."

Then she would have a seizure and end up in the emergency room.

I had to learn to exercise a lot of patience and love with her. I called her every night before I went to bed to remind her to take her medicine. I started going over to the house every other day to check her medicine bottle, and traveled with her to doctor's appointments.

I felt like I was becoming the parent. I was physically and mentally exhausted. Finally Mom got tired of visiting the emergency room and started regularly taking the medicine.

Just when I thought life was returning to

normal, Mom started complaining about excruciating back pain. The doctors could not diagnose her condition. Some days she felt better than others. One night she called me, complaining about not being able to get off the sofa. I told her to call 9-1-1, but she refused. So I called a neighbor and asked her to check. Her neighbor called the ambulance.

My mother stayed in intensive care for one week. She was put on morphine for the pain. My sisters and I took turns staying at her bedside, making sure she was okay. I often turned toward the window and cried. I had never seen my mother in such poor condition, and having to spoon-feed her broke my heart. Of course, my mom had spoon-fed me when I was a child, but I never imagined I would have to do the same for her.

But what greater love can a child show a parent than to return the love given to them? I mused as I learned to take care of Mom's basic needs.

The doctors finally gave us a diagnosis. An infectious disease had invaded her spinal cord system. They started her on a drug regimen through an IV drip. She remained in the hospital for another month.

Because she had to learn to walk again,

Mom was sent to a rehab center for two months. I became her coach as she struggled to regain strength in her legs. Every day I marveled as I watched Mom take baby steps and then walk again with a walker. I rejoiced with her just like I'm sure she did when I learned how to walk.

After three months Mom was excited to come back home. Yet I worried about how she would manage. My fears were soon realized and it was evident that Mom could not live alone anymore.

I spent four days a week at Mom's house, taking care of her, while working full time. It became too much. After much prayer and discussion with my sisters, I knew what had to be done. At the age of forty-one, I resigned from my job, sold my possessions, and moved back home. It was hard to leave the life I had built for myself and return home, but I knew this was the right decision.

I immediately had to relearn how to relate to my mother. Our relationship had changed over the years. I had become my own person. You could say I had cut the apron strings.

Mom struggled with the new me but came to embrace my uniqueness. We started to learn to appreciate each other in a new way.

Just as things were starting to normalize, we received shocking news. Mom was suffering from dementia. The signs were there, but I attributed it to old age, figuring I forget things, too. She was given medication to help her memory, but the doctor warned us her condition would worsen. It has deteriorated over the last year.

In the midst of dementia and the other physical ailments, I have relearned how to love her. I grieve for the mom she used to be, but I embrace the person she is now. I am privileged to be able to teach, remind, and reveal new truths to her.

Yes, it is tough being her caregiver. She goes into the grocery store with me and wanders away. When I find her, she has purchased five bulk packages of toilet paper, eight boxes of trash bags, ten packs of pudding, and three gallons of milk! I have to lovingly remind her that we do not need those items and return them.

Mom often screams that the television is broken when she has turned it off or cannot remember how to use the remote. I have to teach her how to use the remote again and again and again.

She answers the phone and tells people I do not live with her. Mom does not remember how to use the microwave so she tries to turn on the stove to fry a microwave dinner! I have to help her use the microwave every day.

Mom used to teach Bible study at church but cannot remember the lessons anymore. The pastor lets her assist during Bible study and give input.

This is where Mom is at during this part of her life. I can either deny it or readjust accordingly. I have chosen to adjust and learn how to love her in a different way.

The lessons I am learning have forever changed my life. I am no longer self-centered. I have learned how to laugh. I am more patient, compassionate, and forgiving. I rely totally on God for strength. Every day is a new adventure with Mom, and every day is another opportunity to love her.

— *Faith Waters*

People change. Sometimes physical problems change them, as Mrs. Waters' life and personality changed because of dementia. At other times, emotional problems or life challenges make people change. And sometimes people just change because life is fluid.

When people change, we might, like Faith, face a decision. Are we going to let go of the relationship? Or, are we going to learn to love the new person who has entered the body

223

with which we are familiar?

Learning to love new personalities in familiar skin takes courage. It means not only loving who the person was but also embracing who this person has become. As Faith has found, the process of relearning to love may be harder than we ever dreamed possible. But real love has the courage to continue reaching out through the challenges of life.

TRIALS AND ERRORS

Before I got married, someone told me the first year of marriage would be the hardest. When my wife and I celebrated our first anniversary, I reflected on the year and considered whether or not I agreed. I remembered the first time I saw my wife break down. She couldn't find the cucumber slicer and cried in the bedroom for an hour. "I think you're overreacting. Can't you just use a knife?"

"You don't understand," she said. "I don't want to use a knife. I want to use the slicer. I just want to know where it is. I saw it yesterday."

All this over cucumbers? I thought. She was right, I didn't understand.

Several times she called me at work, crying because she'd burned dinner, couldn't find the remote control, or lost her keys. "I have customers lined up to the door. Can I call you on my next break?"

225

"Don't even bother," she'd snap. Then she'd hang up.

Great. I get to work for eight hours, then go home and have one of those three-hour talks.

So at the time I concluded that the first year of marriage had to be the hardest.

The next year, my wife and I tried to start a family. Becoming a mom was my wife's sole ambition. She knew this from the time she got her first baby-sitting gig at the age of eleven. She spent her high school years as the neighborhood couples' first-call for their date nights.

In college, she got a bachelor's degree in child development. Armed with a diploma, sensible wits, and a deep love for well-behaved children, she worked successfully as a full-time nanny for several years. Each family that employed her loved her. The kids saw her as a third parent, and their moms and dads trusted her with credit cards. But as she became more a part of each family, she longed all the more for a family of her own.

Considering her skills and passion, it was one of life's cruel little jokes that she couldn't get pregnant. We tried unsuccessfully for a year before we researched doctors.

I remember the conversation we had many

times before our first visit to a reproductive endocrinologist. "Other couples are able to get pregnant so easily," she always said. "Why is it so hard for us?"

I finally ran out of responses. At some point I gave up and just said, "I don't know, honey."

The next few months dragged on painfully. Our relationship began to suffer. I spent my entire breaks at work listening to her meltdowns.

"You don't understand what I'm going through," she said. "It's *my* body that's broken, not yours. You don't have to go to the clinic every other day for exams and blood tests and sonograms."

While this was true, it's not like I could do anything about it. I couldn't go through the procedures for her. At times I didn't call during breaks because I didn't want to deal with questions I couldn't answer.

About a year into the treatments, my wife and I went to a marriage retreat where we shared an intensive counseling experience with two other couples. Our first assignment was to each create a life map of our experiences, which we would later discuss.

When my wife's turn came, she shared her story of growing up and how she and I first met and fell in love. When we got to the part about our current relationship, she shared about our struggles with infertility and as usual began sobbing.

The leader asked if I had been there for her in her grief. As I waited for her to proclaim my sensitivity to the group, I heard her say, "No."

"When have I not been there for you?" I asked.

"Lots of times."

"Like when?"

"Do you remember a month ago when I couldn't sleep? I cried for hours, and you just lay there and pretended to sleep. Then when I tried to wake you up so you would talk to me, you snapped, 'This again?' Then you kicked the sheets off the bed and stormed out."

"I did that?" I sat back, stunned.

I tried to remember the incident. If she said it happened, I believed her. I was certainly concerned that I was capable of treating my wife so impatiently. But what concerned me more was that I had absolutely no recollection of this incident.

I wracked my brain trying to remember when I had been insensitive to her grief. I recalled evenings I had been watching TV or working on the computer when she wandered in and asked, "What'cha doing?"

"Busy."

"Do you want to do something together?"

This question always irked me. It implied I never spent any time with her. Also, it irritated me that I felt trapped by the possible responses. If I said yes, I'd be spending time with her out of pity. I'd be distracted by what I really wanted to be doing. I'd resent her for taking me away from it, and I'd do a terrible job of hiding it.

If I said no, I'd feel selfish for not wanting to spend time with her. One night I got tired of it and said, "You really need to get a hobby."

Now I realized the message I had sent: *Your pain, your misery, and your identity crisis are a nuisance. You need to get over this and move on, for* my *sake, and get a life.*

Was this the husband I had become?

The counselor turned to me and asked, "How do you feel about what your wife said?"

"These last few months have been really hard on us —"

"No, no," he interrupted. "Don't say it to me. Say it to her."

I turned to my wife. "I know these last few months have been really hard for us, and I guess I didn't know how to handle you when you were sad. I felt incompetent because I couldn't fix our problems."

"Why did you have to fix them? Why couldn't you just listen to me?"

"What good does that do?"

"That's how you can make me feel better. You can just be there for me. I don't need you to always fix my problems. Sometimes I do. But other times, I just need you to listen. You have to take the time to hear me out."

"So you want me to just listen to you when you're sad? And that's how I can be there for you?"

"Exactly."

"How do I do that?"

She thought about it for a second. "I don't know. I guess we'll just have to figure it out together."

When we got back from the retreat, our doctor began preparing us for our most expensive and ambitious treatment — an IUI (Intrauterine Insemination). The procedure's prep included daily injections I had to give my wife in her lower stomach. Also, she had to take multiple medications. She had to go to the clinic every other day for sonograms and blood tests. Her arms began to bruise.

I couldn't get the day off work for the procedure. Later my wife told me how she was lying on the examination table and began to cry. The doctor asked her, "Why are you upset? Most of my patients are really excited about this part."

"It wasn't supposed to happen like this." I guess she didn't know how to tell him that the dream of spending an intimate evening with her spouse and conceiving a child was over.

Two weeks later our pregnancy test came back negative. We could either perform two more IUIs or move on to IVF (In Vitro Fertilization).

That night we didn't say much at dinner. It seemed to me that our grief, instead of tearing us apart, had finally united us and we didn't have anything else to say. Rather than doing anything together, we both just stayed at home.

I couldn't resist the urge to clean. I'd never realized how similar mourning and boredom could be. Doing the dishes and the laundry gave me the control over my life that had otherwise been lost.

I wondered if this was the grief my wife had experienced for the past year. So why was it finally bothering me now? Had I learned from the retreat how to be in the moment with her? Or maybe the treatments hadn't really affected me until now. The doctor gave the IUI a 25 percent success probability. I had let myself think that our year of disappointment would finally change and we would finally get what we had worked so hard for and felt we deserved. Ultimately, I think what I felt that night was my first experience with true grief.

Early the next morning, I woke up and found my wife on the bathroom floor crying. I sat next to her and put my arm on her leg. We didn't say anything for several minutes. We just shared the silence. When she sighed, I sighed. Finally, she whispered, "What are we going to do?"

"We've got to stop the procedures."

"If we stop, then all of our investment in this — the money, the pain, the grief — was a waste. We'll have nothing to show for the past few years."

"I know. But I feel like I'm watching our future slip away. These treatments are like gambling; the more we lose, the more we feel we need to stay with it just to have something to show for it. We've got to stop now before we lose anything else."

We ended our infertility treatments. At the time, I just assumed that the grief and disappointment had finally exhausted us. Years later, my wife told me that she began to heal from the heartbreak when I grieved with her. She told me it wasn't anything complicated — I'd simply made time for her and listened to her and let her vent without correcting her.

I hadn't made a conscious effort to focus on her needs. Rather I made more of an effort to be involved.

As I look back on my first three years of marriage, I think about the really hard times. I think about the emotional pain and loss of dreams we shared and how these affected me as a husband. But I also see how similar these experiences are to the cucumber slicer and the burnt dinners. In the moment, my wife needs the same thing from me — to listen to her and validate her feelings.

These experiences we've shared have played a significant role in the kind of family I now have. We have grown closer and more intimate than I ever thought I could be with another human. My ability to be involved has strengthened my relationship with my wife . . . and it's helped me be the type of father to my two adopted children that I can be proud of.

— *Billy Cuchens*

Many of us are created to want to solve problems or "fix" everything for those we love.

And when we can't, we become frustrated and impatient. Sometimes, if we're honest, we have to admit that if we can't fix the problem, we don't want to be bothered.

Love doesn't require that we always have all the answers. Instead, many times love just asks that we listen to the problem, that we try to understand, and that we express our condolences, sympathy, or love.

Sometimes love means just being there for the person we care about — trying to feel what that one is experiencing emotionally; listening and learning her perspective until we start to understand and feel compassion. As Billy found, love often means simply "living in the moment" with another person.

IT'S NOT ABOUT ME

"I feel like a princess!" I exclaimed to my friend and matron of honor as we discussed my plans for the wedding. At the monthly game night she and her husband hosted a year earlier, I had met Dave. He was a thirty-five-year-old bachelor, and I was a thirty-two-year-old widow with three young children, two still in diapers.

Mutual friends had told me stories of the many women who had tried to win Dave. They also warned that he would never marry a woman with three children. Yet he chose to ask me to marry him! Seven months later, we stood at the altar vowing, "Absolutely!" to love and to cherish.

It was especially meaningful that Dave chose to marry me over all those other women, because I had lived with feelings of rejection and inadequacy for a long time. When my first husband died, we had been in the process of repairing a broken marriage after years of hurts.

I had learned a lot in my first marriage and had resolved that if I remarried, everything, including the type of man, would be different. I realized I played a part in the discord we experienced in that marriage, but I believed my husband was mostly to blame.

Dave was definitely different. Unlike my first husband, he had great problem-solving and contingency-planning abilities. I admired and respected those qualities . . . I thought.

After we decided to get married, the plans jelled quickly. We wanted to get married in seven months. I efficiently reserved the church, obtained a choir, and began to gather prices and information about the key components needed for a reasonably inexpensive but nice wedding.

When I felt I had ample information to share with Dave, we sat down to review what I thought were well-developed lists of things I had done. After I proudly presented the information, he responded, "So who has the key to get into the church that morning?"

"Well, I don't know right now, but I'm sure when we get closer to the time we'll know," I replied.

"I think we should know that now so we aren't standing outside the church unable to get in."

"We have months to figure that out. I can't believe you're going to make a big deal about such a minute detail!"

I was frustrated about Dave's focus on something seemingly so unimportant at the time. I was also hurt because of what I thought he was really saying: *You failed at this task.*

Within the first few years of our marriage, we encountered quite a few instances like that in which I walked away feeling inadequate or like a failure.

Once, Dave came into the kitchen while I was cutting a hardboiled egg and said, "You're cutting it the wrong way."

I asked him what the right way was and he showed me. I was irritated that he could make something so nebulous a right-or-wrong issue.

Another time I heard the vacuum cleaner and inquired, "Honey, what are you doing?"

"I'm vacuuming our room."

"Why are you vacuuming? Did it look like it needed to be vacuumed?"

"I thought I would help out."

"I do the vacuuming; you don't have to do it for me," I replied, annoyed. I interpreted his saying he would help as "You're not doing your job so I'm doing it for you." Again, I felt he was saying I was inadequate.

Another example came at the end of a workday, when Dave attentively asked, "So how was your day?"

I shared the frustration I felt with a situation at work. Instead of understanding and listening, he started giving me possible solutions. I thought I was already handling the situation and just needed to vent. I felt he was telling me I was incapable of figuring out a solution on my own.

I knew Dave loved me, but I wasn't feeling loved. Instead, I felt hurt and inadequate. Although Dave was a completely different man from my first husband, I was experiencing similar feelings as I'd felt in my first marriage. How could this be?

After repeatedly working through those kinds of situations, I discovered both my marriages had a common factor — ME.

Through some deep soul-searching, I realized I saw those circumstances as being about me and took whatever Dave said or did too personally.

In working through the hurts from my first marriage and other relationships, I had become accustomed to analyzing how life affected *me*. Blind to the fact that life was not just about me, I was too sensitive to my surroundings, especially to those closest to me. I realized I was an adult, but emotionally my reactions were childish and definitely not beneficial to me, or my marriage.

I was looking for my husband to acknowledge and appreciate those things I did well. Yet Dave admits he does not readily notice or acknowledge things that have already been completed and done well. He is more apt to look for things that need to be finished or fixed. Instead of appreciating Dave's problem-solving abilities, I took his attempts to be helpful as personal offenses.

In each scenario, Dave was only trying to be helpful, not make a judgment on my character or performance. In each, I only needed to hear the information and to decide what to do with it.

Dave's question about the key was a legitimate question. He was merely thinking ahead, not making a statement about my ability to plan. The fact that I hadn't thought of the key at that point certainly did not make me a failure. I could have simply acknowledged the oversight, added the question to my ongoing list, and moved on. Instead, I made it all about me.

Loving my husband includes giving him the freedom to help, give advice, and share his thoughts without interpreting his intentions as personal attacks. Loving him is accepting that his attempts to help are just that — attempts to help. Loving him is taking the focus off me and hearing him with understanding and acceptance. It's letting him know I appreciate his input, and even telling him when his suggestions are useful.

Recently, I showed him a piece I wrote to advertise a program at our church. I wanted his feedback on whether I'd clearly communicated what the program was about. As he read, he began to question the structure of the program.

At one time I would have become defensive since I had developed the program structure. I would have reminded him to pay attention only to what I'd asked him to focus on. Instead, I listened to his viewpoint and we discussed our thought processes. I walked away from that conversation not completely convinced of his opinion but willing to consider it.

As I thought about it, I realized that he had some good points, and I made changes that incorporated his thoughts. Afterward I thanked him for his input and I let him know I did implement his suggestions. In this incident, I was able to demonstrate love toward my husband by respectfully listening to and even considering his ideas without making it about me.

Taking the focus off me in these types of situations opens the door for me to more readily accept and overlook Dave's short-comings — and helps me appreciate and respect him. I am able to love him with a more genuine love.

— Christine McNamara

The young adults of the 1980s were often referred to as the selfish or the "Me" generation. Unfortunately, that segment of the population at that time in history didn't have a corner on the self-focused market.

In fact, in homes, schools, companies, and even churches, we're becoming increasingly focused on "making sure my needs are being met." If they aren't, we're outta there — to that elusive person, place, or organization that will be "better" for us. We seek to be served rather than to serve. As a result, we end up always on the go instead of settling down with maturity and letting our roots deepen in our relationships.

As Christine learned, "It's not about me." Instead, the best relationships are those in which we decide that everything should revolve around the other person.

It's strange, but in life, as the old-timers said,

"What goes around comes around." As we become less self-focused and start focusing on others in our relationships, sometimes they start focusing on us. And that's when the roots of love grow down deep, find nourishment, and start to flower.

Not the Girl for My Son?

Slowly opening my eyes, I tried to focus on the tiny bundle placed in my arms.

"It's a boy," the nurse said. "And he has a full head of hair."

It was love at first sight!

Growing up in a family of four girls, I longed for a male offspring. My whole extended family was thrilled that we finally had a little boy in our midst.

As Trant grew, he was always surrounded by adoring loved ones. He could do no wrong in his relatives' eyes. Trant excelled in the classroom. He had many friends and enjoyed participating in any sport.

All during Trant's growing-up years, I consistently prayed for, and imagined, what kind of wife my son would need. As he got older he brought many attractive young girls home for me to meet. I liked most of them very much.

No matter how cute or sweet these girls

were, though, Trant never dated one very long. By the time he enrolled in college he had never had a steady girlfriend.

One day he told me he'd dreamed a few nights earlier about a dark-eyed, dark-haired girl. After he explained the entire dream, I agreed that maybe a woman really was out there like the one in the dream, a woman who'd be perfect for him.

I had no idea he was about to find her. In fact, my youngest sister introduced them, or rather, reintroduced them. They had briefly worked together while she was still married. Karen's husband had become involved with another woman and had left her and their two young daughters.

Karen was not my ideal for my son. At first, I convinced myself that their attraction was based on his compassion for her and the children and her need for help. But I had never seen my son so smitten. Suddenly he wanted to spend every minute with her.

The children, ages two and five, were delightful, but I still was not happy about the courtship. My son was still in college and could hardly look after himself much less take on a family. To top it off, in the midst of this drama, I completely lost my voice and could not utter a sound.

One day the phone rang and my husband

told me our son wanted to talk to me. Trant knew I couldn't answer him, so I couldn't imagine why he called me. I picked up the phone and whistled faintly, because that was all I could do.

"Mama," he exclaimed, "I've just asked Karen to marry me. What do you think?"

There was silence because I was truly speechless in every sense of the word.

"Mom," he continued, "if you're happy about it, whistle once, or if you aren't whistle twice."

I was so overcome with emotion I could barely squeak a faint whistle, much less a second one. He was overjoyed. "Mom, I knew you'd be happy about it." Then I heard him tell Karen, "Mother thinks it's wonderful, too!"

When I got off the phone, I sobbed. I grabbed my notepad that I kept with me due to my voiceless condition and wrote a note to my husband explaining the phone call. He put his arms around me and assured me that everything would work out for the best.

That night I tossed and turned, trying to find a way to deal with this problem. In my mind, I thought about all the reasons why it wouldn't work out.

The next day I realized my husband was

right — we needed to make the best of this. But I simply did not know how to do it.

The more I tried to discuss the situation with my husband and close friends, the more impossible the problem seemed. Every time Trant brought Karen to our house, I sensed that she was nervous and unsure of herself around me.

One night I began listing all the negative things about their relationship. After I filled a page, to be fair, I thought I would also write anything good about their upcoming union. The only thing I could think of for that page was to write that the two little girls were darling.

Day after day I focused on my distress regarding their relationship. I was being consumed by grief. Then one morning as I looked over my list again, I wrote, "She is a good mother and she has dark hair and eyes."

Well, that wasn't much, but it was a start.

As soon as I determined that I had to change the way I felt about this girl my son had set his heart on, something truly incredible began to happen. I stopped tossing and turning at night and was able to get some real sleep again.

The true turning point in my relationship with Karen, however, happened one Sunday afternoon. My husband and I had just come in from eating out after church. Since Trant's car was in the driveway, as we opened the front door, I called out to him to let him know we were home. We had a special guest with us, a prominent attorney from Virginia. I wanted our son to meet our friend, but I had no idea Karen was with him.

As I walked into the den, I spotted the two of them. Trant was sprawled in our recliner and Karen was seated on our small couch. They had just returned from the beach and looked like "beach bums." Karen's hair was a wreck, and she didn't have a speck of makeup on. I sensed her insecurity as we introduced our guest, and a lump formed in my throat.

Just then Trant sprang to his feet to hug me, and I turned to also embrace Karen. Looking into her eyes, I was reminded of a tiny rabbit caught in someone's headlights.

As I bent toward her, she rose to greet me. The second she was in my arms I knew a true miracle had just happened. My mother's heart went out to her, and the purest form of love for her engulfed me. I no longer cared what our influential guest thought of her.

That afternoon Karen became my

daughter-in-law. I helped her with her wedding plans, and at her bridesmaids' luncheon I told the guests how much I had learned to love her.

Instead of becoming a stumbling block for my son, Karen became an asset. When Trant decided to go to law school, she helped support the family. When at last Trant graduated from law school with top honors, Karen stood right beside him, and that seemed symbolic. He would have never made it without her.

Looking over the last several years, there have been many of our son's friends who have gone through divorce, but not Trant and Karen. This past January they celebrated their twentieth anniversary. I'm so glad I woke up and realized I couldn't choose a mate for my son; it was always his choice. And after all, he really does have good taste.

— Ann Varnum

We cannot control anyone else in relationship situations. We cannot control the lives of the people we love, nor can we control their choices if they're adults. But we can pray for the best.

When someone we love chooses a romantic interest, we can try to see the person through our loved one's eyes.

Sometimes we just have to trust . . . to believe that the one we care for knows what he is doing. And when we love enough to trust and to pray for the best, we usually aren't disappointed. When we're willing to have our initial opinions changed, we're often pleasantly surprised.

SILVER-BOXED
KINDNESS

My husband hadn't been home from work more than fifteen minutes when he said something that poured lighter fuel on my fiery emotions. I don't even remember what he said now. But I *can* recall my response.

Unfortunately for Rodney, I'd been rehearsing a sentence that had roared through my mind like wildfire ever since our unresolved argument about the electric bill that morning.

"I wish I was one of your clients!" I snapped. My palms grew clammy.

I bit my lip. If Rodney could see that the people he worked with got exactly what *I* wanted — a listening ear, a word of encouragement or advice, someone to fight their battles, laugh with, and walk alongside — he'd feel bad about all the ways he ignored my needs.

He rolled his tongue along the inside of his cheek, frowned, and scrutinized me through half-lidded eyes.

"And that means?" I hate it when my attorney husband plays the prosecutor, leading his witness like he's clueless — something you're not supposed to do in a real court *or* the court of marriage.

My hands flew to my hips, and I heard my voice whine, "Then you'd treat me with respect."

"I come home from the war zone to enter another. I can't win." He flipped the air-conditioner to chilly as if the heated air between us hadn't already turned frigid.

With lightning-bolt clarity I realized if I really wanted respect, I probably should show some. But I didn't have time to ponder the thought before he irritated me again.

"I'll be at the golf course," he said, and walked out.

Talk about a cycle destined to incinerate the sturdiest of marriages. The more he ignored my needs, the more I complained; and the more he withdrew, the more I punished him. Then he'd complain that I wasn't encouraging enough, and I'd protest some more. Didn't he realize there was no way to encourage a man like him? I sighed. At least our children hadn't been present this time.

I met a friend for lunch the next day. Joy had recently returned home from a mission trip abroad and was eager to catch up. It didn't take long for my marital problems to spill out.

Although perfectly matched to a mellow mate, Joy barely batted an eye as she absorbed my ire. When she prayed for me, I felt distracted. But one thing she said captured my attention: "Let Pam's words to Rodney be like silver boxes of encouragement."

I had no time to ask what she meant by such an odd sentence. I rushed off to carpool. The catchphrase "silver boxes of encouragement" rolled around my brain like a seedling dropped on charred soil; a picture of a different life struggled to sprout.

I decided to find a silver box to fill with supportive words. Although I wasn't sure I'd be able to do it, or find a box, I had to try.

"I want to be more encouraging to Daddy," I told my three daughters when they climbed into the minivan.

They argued that their dad didn't deserve it, justifying my desire to turn back from my impulsive idea. The months of ongoing verbal sparring had gotten to all of us, and I wavered.

Swallowing my pride hurt, but I managed to say, "You don't have to encourage Daddy unless you want to, but be patient with me as I try. This experiment might help us all."

I tried to explain my nebulous plan while I parked in front of a small gift shop. "You want to come in and help me look?" The twins had homework to do, so I plunged inside with my ten-year-old in tow.

"Look, Mamma, there's your box." Lindsay pointed to a lone silver box on a curio table and then dashed to the kids' section.

I found five other silver boxes in the back of the store. I opened each to find a red velvet lining. I frowned. Something about the color red reminded me of what I'd be giving up by changing — the *power* to harp and complain, the *right* to take his bait and react with vengeance, the *entitlement* that shouted I didn't deserve to be treated this way.

I shook my head. I was as filled with ugly thinking as my husband was with unbridled anger.

I returned to examine the box my daughter had picked out. This little treasure box had white velvet lining that reminded me of what I wanted my words to represent: sincere kindness.

When we got home, I placed the box on

my bathroom counter beneath the mirror. That might sound silly, but I figured I'd have to practice saying anything I came up with. The situation was that bad between us. The task of encouraging a man who'd made my life miserable took on the proportions of a miracle. I tapped my pencil, pondering what to say. What sincere compliment could I offer?

I finally wrote on a strip of paper: "I appreciate it when you fill up the gas tank."

I slipped the sentence into the box and decided to tell Rodney when we were all alone. I didn't want to see the girls rolling their eyes.

I spoke the simple words with a pounding heart. He said, "Thank you for noticing."

Wow. My skin tingled.

As I slid beneath the comforter to read a verse or two from the Bible before bed, I found Ephesians 4:29: "Let everything you say be good and helpful, so that your words will be an encouragement to those who hear them." I smiled as I drifted off to sleep with a *thank-you* winging heavenward.

Throughout the next year, I filled the silver box with many encouraging words. Rodney had no idea what I was doing, but his attitude changed, and he seemed to gain more confidence. The girls noticed too.

Peace had entered our home.

I spoke and wrote until the sentences popped out of the box like springy jack-in-the-box papers. It was heartening to watch my experiment grow.

When I got discouraged, I would reread my positive comments to bolster my resolve. As I practiced dispensing encouragement, it became more ingrained.

On New Year's Day, I presented the silver box to Rodney. He painstakingly opened each narrow strip of paper — at least two hundred. He read them aloud, stunned. He hadn't realized I'd been filling a box, but he had noticed *I'd* changed!

— *Pamela Dowd*

Words are powerful and compliments are strong. The Bible even talks about words well spoken being like "golden apples in a silver basket" (Proverbs 25:11). Gold and silver are not only precious metals but also valuable.

Likewise, complimentary words are not only precious but valuable. One sweet comment may not make a lot of difference, but add up enough of them — at least one a day — and they can stem the negative tide in a relationship and even change the direction.

The key, as Pamela pointed out, is sincerity. When we're just flattering someone, they usually see through it or mistrust the lack of honesty they sense. But when we're vulnerable, specific, and truthful, our words are appreciated.

Don't know where to start in bringing compliments into a relationship? Well, something as basic as "I appreciate it when you fill up the gas tank," as Pamela found, works just fine.

A Spring Tulip in Frozen Ground

When I was twenty-one, I married my best friend, Jack. We met at college. I loved him for his good sense of humor, his wit, and his easygoing personality. He was voted class clown, and daily he made me laugh out loud. It was his trademark. He also seemed stable and faithful, two qualities I counted most valuable since I grew up in a broken home. I thought my love for him would last forever, but we were young and our love was built on the unrealistic expectations we had for each other.

At the seven-year mark of our marriage, I watched my husband's personality change from a self-confident man of great charm to an unhappy man, a difficult-to-live-with stranger. And as he changed, I found myself losing my love for him.

We had just moved from California back to our college town of Spokane, Washington, planning to raise our young family there.

Although Jack didn't have a job, we had saved enough money for several weeks' living expenses and felt confident that he would find a job soon.

We were wrong.

"You're overeducated," employer after employer told him, looking at his two degrees in psychology and theology. There were no openings where he could utilize his academic training. Employers in blue-collar jobs were reluctant to hire him, afraid he'd leave when something better opened up.

As employment doors continued to close, Jack withdrew deeper into himself. He'd roam restlessly around the house brooding, not talking to any of us.

When our three-year-old daughter would ask, "Daddy, please play with me," he'd snap at her, "Don't bother me, I'm thinking." Her daddy's behavior confused her. Normally he loved to romp and play with her.

When I'd ask, "Do you want to talk about what's bothering you?" I'd get a curt brush-off: "Nothing's bothering me" or "I don't want to talk."

When I suggested something the family could do together like a picnic in the park, he'd respond, "I'd rather not . . . go by yourselves." Always a whistler, he even stopped that. He just brooded in introspective silence.

I began to respond to Jack's bad moods. They made me angry. I started giving him all kinds of advice about how he could find work.

"Honey," I said to him one day, "why don't you sell vacuum cleaners? They're always looking for sales representatives."

Yet as I said it I knew full well he had a phobia about that kind of door-to-door selling.

I gave him all kinds of spiritual advice, too. "You're trying to carry this all by yourself," I'd say, expecting him to "rest in the Lord," and to enjoy each day with the family.

As weeks dragged into months, I became disgusted with his behavior. Jack was no longer the joyful, loving man I had married. An icy distance grew wider and wider between us, and to make matters worse we fell two months behind in the rent. Our savings were all gone.

Now I felt helplessly trapped. I kept trying to blot out the ugly thought of divorce. I didn't want to leave Jack, but I also didn't want to stay with him. The very idea of divorce saddened me. My mother had been married three times, and I lived with the memory of a premarital counselor warning me that statistically I, too, was a divorce risk. "It's almost inevitable for you," he had said.

To me, divorce seemed like a kind of death, a black empty room with no light or life. I'd experienced its pain too much with my own parents and yet I couldn't imagine living for a lifetime with someone I didn't love.

One afternoon when I felt at my lowest ebb, my next-door neighbor dropped in. I'd enjoyed wonderful over-the-fence conversations with Peg. She'd been married many years, and we often shared our thoughts on family and faith. She had become a motherly presence for me.

We sat at the kitchen table. I poured cups of tea. There was a silence. Then Peg spoke: "How are you doing, Gena? How are you really doing?"

Something in her gentle tone triggered my pent-up feelings. I blurted out, "I don't know what I'm going to do, Peg. I don't love Jack anymore!"

"Oh, that," she replied calmly. I felt hurt at the matter-of-fact way she took my startling confession.

Peg put her hand on mine. "Gena, I've been watching you two young people. What you are feeling about Jack is nothing unexpected, or new. It's happened to me and many other women, as well."

"But this is different," I protested.

"No, my dear, I'm afraid it's not." And then Peg began to give me the wisest lesson in loving that I'd ever heard. "Human love is a living thing, always changing," she began. "It changes as we change, and sometimes we shape it ourselves. We put conditions on it, such as 'I'll love you if you meet my expectations.' "

As she talked I began to wonder, had I lost my love for Jack because he was no longer the cheerful man I'd married?

"But there's one love that doesn't change," Peg added. "And that's the one you have to bring into your marriage now."

"What love is that?" I asked, a little bewildered.

"It's God's resurrection love. When our human love dies, He can replace it with divine love."

Before Peg went home that day, she urged me to pray and ask God for His love for Jack, but first I must be willing to trust Him, to wait to see what He could do. She encouraged me to see Jack as God sees him, with understanding, tenderness, forbearance, and forgiveness.

As soon as Peg left for home, I spoke out loud the simplest prayer, "God, I ask you to give me your love for Jack."

A few hours later, Jack came home, his face revealing the discouragement of his day. *Who has turned him down this time?* I wondered. *What kind of painful rejection is he feeling now?*

For the first time in weeks I looked at him without trying to avoid his eyes, and as I did, I felt a little surge of warmth, like a blade of a green spring tulip forcing its way from the frozen ground of winter.

From that day on, it seemed to me that Jack began to change. What I didn't grasp then, however, was that *I* was the one who was changing. I stopped trying to exert my will on him, stopped trying to make him meet my expectations. I left him to find his own way while I stopped the nagging. I concentrated on taking good care of the children and doing my best to say and think only genuinely supportive things. And I prayed often to God that He would watch over my husband.

About a week later, when we were down to our very last five dollars, Jack unexpectedly called the children and me into the living room. We gathered around the fireplace.

"I want to read something to you," he

explained, "and tell you what I've done." As I sat with our one-year-old squirming on my lap, he read to us the passage in Matthew 6:25–26 that says, "Do not worry about your life, what you will eat . . ." (NIV), and continues with the assurance that if God cares for the birds of the air, surely He will care for us.

"I told God," Jack said, "that since this is His promise to us, I must believe He will take care of me and my family. I've tried with my own strength to find a job using every avenue I know. I've found nothing and have no prospects.

"Well, God," Jack continued, "I trust you now to do what's best for all of us. Until you do, I'm going to pretend that I'm on vacation and enjoy the time with my family."

And with that announcement he looked around at us and smiled, really smiled, for the first time in months!

The next morning, buoyant with his conviction of God's loving care, Jack decided to look once more for work. He told us later that as he drove toward town, he prayed again, "God, please guide me. I don't know where else to go." At that very moment, his eyes were drawn to a sign advertising the one employment agency he hadn't visited. He entered the office and behind the main desk found a college friend he hadn't seen for years.

After he poured out the story of his frustrating search for work, his friend told him about an entry-level job with the state of Washington. Jack was hired. It was a low-paying job, but it was a job, and Jack gave all his energy to it. Within three years his responsibilities and salary had tripled.

Jack stayed with state work for thirty-six years, supporting his growing family of four children through college and into careers of their own. He was promoted to a job within the state that used his degrees earned in college. To this day, he counsels men in recovery.

We are now grandparents! We are also enjoying a relationship with each other far better than ever. The love and joy, the humor and faithfulness, has come from the knowledge of God's unconditional love for both of us and from the lessons we've learned about showing grace to each other, forgiving one another because we are forgiven by God. All we needed to do was ask the Father of life to take a dead relationship and make something brand-new.

Together we have experienced the supernatural power of God's resurrection love, a love that has grown through all the years of our marriage. Each trial became an opportunity to learn to love God's way.

Just when you think love is at an end, that's the time to really start loving. As Peg would say, that's the time to tap into the love that is always there and never changes — God's love.

— *Gena Bradford*

Relationships, like life in general, go through seasons. Sometimes we're in arid summer seasons when our relationships seem dry and in need of some nurturing rain. Sometimes we go through harvest times of plenty, when feasting and thankfulness are in order. At other times, our relationships are cold, and it's hard to keep the flames fanned. Sometimes we even think our friendships or relationships are facing a wintry death.

But like a plant that bursts from the cold ground grows and blooms every spring, if we have planted love, we can be sure our relationships will eventually find new life. Sometimes it just means hanging in there during the cold, dark days when we forget what the warmth of life is like.

If you're feeling the icy winds, hang on with love . . . soon the season will change.

ALL SHE NEEDED
WAS TIME

On our twenty-fifth wedding anniversary, my husband left me alone to care for his ninety-three-year-old mother. She had lived in our home for two years, and some days were easier than others. When I delivered her breakfast to her room, I checked her bedding and snagged her dirty pants from the chair before she could put them on again.

"Grandma, it's just an hour until the visiting nurse comes. She'll help you bathe."

"I don't need anyone to help me," she snarled at me. "If you hadn't tricked my son into marrying you, I wouldn't be here."

Tears filled my eyes. I turned my back on the angry white-haired woman and opened her closet. "I washed your lavender dress yesterday. Do you want to wear it or the pink one?"

"I told everyone if you were good to me, I'd give you my tablecloth. Well, no daughter-in-law is ever going to treat me this way. You can't make me have a bath."

I didn't stay to listen to the rest of her tirade. I scooted into the bathroom before tears of self-pity rained down my face. "Lord, I've done everything to make that woman like me. What do I do now?"

Before long, I'd mopped my face, retouched my makeup, and met the nurse at the back door. I used her visit as an opportunity to run an errand and tried to leave the cloud of depression behind.

At the store, my friend Tammy's cheerfulness brought a fresh bucket of tears.

"Good morning, Kathy. How are things with Grandma?" She handed me a tissue and said, "That bad?"

"Married twenty-five years today, you'd think I'd be used to whatever that woman might say."

"You're a saint, you know."

"No saint. I'm selfish. I keep hoping our kids are taking lessons and will take care of me when I'm old."

Tammy laughed.

"My mother-in-law is an incredibly strong woman and will probably outlive me."

As I left the store, I thought back to the very beginning.

"My mother wants to see you." Gary had

ushered me to the back of the sanctuary. "Mom, this is Kathy. I'll drive the car to the front of the church."

Gary left me, a painfully shy fifteen-year-old scrawny brunette, standing with a woman a full head taller than me. Her shock of white curly hair framed her wrinkled face. Her austerity was intimidating.

"Well, since my son seems intent on seeing you, I guess we'd better be friends." She shoved her gloved hand toward me. "We'll be riding to church together from now on."

"Yes, ma'am."

"You are invited for Sunday dinner next week."

"Yes, ma'am."

The pastor and his wife stood at the front door when we walked down the stairs. I wondered if I looked as terrified as I felt.

Outside, Gary opened the passenger door and motioned us in. His mother scooted across the bench seat to the middle of the two-door Ford coupe.

The next Sunday when Gary arrived at my house, he whispered, "I'll open my door, and you slide in the middle."

I didn't look at his mother, but her stiffness told me she didn't like what had just happened.

My first meal in Gary's home was an old-fashioned Sunday dinner, consisting of pot roast, carrots, potatoes, and homemade noodles. Mrs. Crawford's apple pie not only looked perfect, it tasted better than anything I'd ever eaten. I knew I'd never be able to cook like this woman. My shyness kept me from doing more than saying please and thank you when necessary.

Gary and I married two years later. We soon learned from a friend at church that Gary's mom had said, "Kathy isn't my choice for my son. I doubt they'll stay married six months."

Still married eight months later, Gary and I moved a hundred miles away.

I'd never called his mother anything, certainly never her first name, *Myrtle.* Now she was my mother-in-law, older than my grandmother. I couldn't call her *Mom, Mama,* or *Mother.* It didn't feel right. After the birth of our first child, my mother visited us for a few days and then Gary's mother arrived. That's when I started calling her *Grandma.*

Although Grandma had seven boys, my husband was her favorite son. Her sons all married, and it seemed to me that she loved "Little Ann" best of the daughters-in-law. She talked constantly about Ann's culinary skills, her perfection in housekeeping, and what a sweet wife and mother she made.

No matter what I did, I couldn't measure up. I learned to keep a neat house and to cook reasonably good meals, but I never received a compliment from Grandma. When she mentioned a perfume she liked, I bought it for her. Later I found she never opened it.

When she complained her purse had worn out, I bought her a new one. Two years later Grandma sent it to me, gift-wrapped for Christmas — a little used. When long skirts were popular, Grandma mentioned how much she liked them. I pulled out the sewing machine and made her a stylish skirt. She wore it twice and brought it back to me.

"Don't like it," she said, crushing my spirit.

When Grandma needed 24/7 care, none of her boys wanted to put her in a nursing home, but none would take care of her either. Since Gary served as pastor and our 900-square-foot apartment was in the church, I had the perfect opportunity to say, "Forget it." Instead, I heard myself saying, "We'll manage somehow."

Neither Gary nor I realized how frightened Grandma might be on the main floor of a new home while we slept upstairs. The first night I heard her labored breathing, ran down the stairs, and called the EMT squad. Grandma was surprised I could hear her.

Many nights after that, I lay on one end of the sectional where she slept while she sat upright on the other. She seemed to enjoy our time together, talking about her childhood years and reminiscing about dogs her boys had owned. Tired, I found myself saying "uh-huh" instead of really hearing her, but still she always thanked me for being there.

With Grandma setting up her home in our living room, every parishioner who visited chatted with her. She always hauled out a beautiful tablecloth she'd crocheted in 1938, and we'd used at our wedding. "Took me a year to make this; Kathy wants it when I die because it's in her wedding pictures. If she's good enough to me, she'll get it."

Some guests thought Grandma was cute. I found the jibes painful.

Then on our twenty-fifth wedding anniversary, Grandma repeated what she'd alluded to when we married: "Never thought you'd stick around this long."

A few days later one of Gary's older brothers and his wife, from another state, visited us. Afterward I learned Grandma had sent

271

the coveted tablecloth home with them with instructions to send it to another brother.

I bawled for hours, until Gary snuggled me into his shoulder and said, "What were you going to do with it anyway? You can't take it to heaven, and it's too full of holes to use."

"I just don't understand. I do this and that and whatever to make her like me."

"Don't *do*. Just be you, because she needs someone to care."

I got over my hurt feelings and did my best to love her. I watched *Wheel of Fortune* with her, took her to the card shop, and helped her thread needles so she could embroider each of her boys one more set of pillowcases.

Grandma finished those pillowcases on a Friday. On Monday Gary said, "Mom doesn't seem quite right today. See what you think."

I took her to the doctor. He asked her the usual questions, then about her family and what she enjoyed doing. Grandma answered every question clearly.

Out of her hearing, he said to me, "She's doing well for ninety-three. I'd say she's probably had a slight stroke. She's fine for the moment, but the next one might be a bad one."

For two days none of the family could entice Grandma to eat. Finally on Thursday afternoon, I spent the last of our grocery money buying the fixings for her favorite meal — fresh green beans, fresh strawberries, and Kentucky Fried Chicken with biscuits and gravy. The whole family sat in her room with her and reminisced while she ate. She finished most of her food and then smiled at me and said, "Thank you. That was the best dinner you ever cooked."

Grandma thought herself quite funny, and I finally did too.

She died the next morning.

That summer Gary and I drove across several states to spend time with his brothers. My sisters-in-law confessed their jealousy. "All we ever heard is how you cook, bake, and sew, and about all the gifts you bought her. She wrote letters about the time you stayed up nights with her, and took her shopping, too. Grandma bragged on you all the time."

"You've gotta be kidding me!" I announced.

On that visit I learned a lot of the family history and how little I knew about my mother-in-law. Then I grieved. I didn't appreciate her until she was gone.

Because I needed acceptance, I gave my

mother-in-law gifts and did things for her. I think above all else she wanted someone — me or Gary or the grandchildren or anyone — to spend time with her.

Some might say I learned Grandma's love language too late. Not that I ever think we'd have been best friends, but after her death I realized Grandma's favorite son, my husband, needed me to freely give her my time. Grandma taught me a lesson of love after all.

— Katherine J. Crawford

Katherine's husband, Gary, gave her some wise words: "Instead of trying to do, just be you, because she needs someone to care."

We live in a "do" focused world. We think if we work hard enough and do all the right things, we'll earn someone's love. Sometimes we wear ourselves out trying to gain approval and trying to prove that we care. We're so busy "doing" for others that we don't have the time to just be with them, to get to know them as a person, and to enjoy their companionship.

So many times people don't want us bustling around like busy bees on their behalf. Instead, if they could be vulnerable and verbalize their feelings, they would admit that they'd much rather we just spend time with them.

Let's stop "doing" and focus on just "being" with someone we love this week.

THE DAY MY
HUSBAND PRAYED I'D
DIE

I did not realize how much my husband
loved me until he prayed I would die.

His love had always been there. But I
don't know that I'd ever really trusted it.
After all, I'd loved my mom, and she had a
history of running away. When I was nine,
she ran away a month before Christmas and
did not come home till many months later.
No one knew where she was or if she was
even alive. My little sister had her first
birthday, and still no mom. We never knew
if she would come back.

My mom married four times. Dad married five times. I was a daddy's girl, in
between his marriages. That left me with
little faith in marriage, or lasting relationships, for that matter.

I mostly lived with my mom, until she left
me a "good-bye, happy birthday" note two
weeks before I turned fifteen. With the note
was my birthday present, a new set of lug-

gage. She wrote, "Be gone before I get home from work."

I went to school crying all the way on a city bus. School was a safe place to hide and pretend this had not happened. But it had, and I had no place to go, so I called my girlfriend. Her mom let me move in with them.

I married the first man who asked me. I didn't know if I loved him. All I wanted in a husband was someone to love me. My husband, Bruce, wanted someone to love, so it worked for us.

Ours was a lopsided marriage. He always wanted to show his love. He would offer kisses and I would brush him away — especially in public. I could not let the neighbors see any display of affection. It would be embarrassing.

I was too busy for hugs or sweet words with Bruce. I was trying to be a super mom and gave my children all the attention. Birthdays and Christmases were always special events planned for months in advance. I had no time to pamper my husband. I figured he was a grown man and he could take care of himself. After all, we are only children for a short time, and I wanted my children to have the best childhood I could give them. To do this, my husband had to work long hours, and I never told him I appreciated it.

I was busy working outside the home and doing many other projects when I encountered a major roadblock: physical pain. I had rheumatoid arthritis. I soon learned that dealing with any chronic disease is a battle. People I knew started telling me their horror stories. Someone had a friend who died of the disease. Another friend told me how long her mother and her family suffered. My best friend researched rheumatoid arthritis and reluctantly told me there was no cure.

These conversations continued for months. No one gave me any hope. There was never any good news.

Because of the pain, I couldn't sleep. Your mind plays tricks on you when you go without sleep. As if the pain were not enough, no sleep made fighting back so much more difficult. Each day seemed to last forever.

As the disease progressed, I grieved my loss of simple daily functions. Things such as tying my shoes and brushing my teeth became struggles that I sometimes left undone. I could not lift my arms. I would squeeze the shampoo in the shower by pressing it against the windowsill with my elbow, then not be able to lift my arms to wash my hair. One day I had to walk down the street to find a neighbor to open my front door. I did not have the strength to turn the handle. Lifting the phone required major effort.

My husband took over all the household chores, even the laundry. I discovered that I no longer cared how many clothes he put in one load, whether he put towels with sweaters and dress pants. When you are in pain, those details suddenly aren't important.

I had to learn how to let go of control and release my desire to have everything perfect. I'd always felt the children had to be perfect so everyone would know I was a good mom. The house had to be perfect in case someone came by. And of course I thought these things could only happen if I did them. That was me — always trying to please everyone . . . except Bruce.

Gradually I found new respect for this partner of mine. I knew he loved me, but I was afraid to love him, and most of all I was afraid to show him I loved him. In some warped way I was afraid that if I showed him too much love, he would not work as hard to show me that he loved me. I needed to know he loved me because I never thought anyone could.

Years before, I'd thought as long as I had supper on the table, his clothes washed, and a clean house, I was a good wife. I never thought he needed time with me. Then everything changed. The children did not need me like before, and they had no time for me in my illness. How could I expect them to neglect their families in order to look in on me? I'd taught them well that children come first.

I was wrong.

When they were young, my children did need love and attention, but so did my husband.

I started realizing who was there for me: God, and the husband He gave me.

I did not want to be dependent on Bruce. It wasn't fair. I had never been there for him emotionally as he was for me. He should not have to wait on me, yet he was there, helping every way he could, and loving me through my pain.

During this most difficult time, Bruce had started a new job, so it was hard for him to take time from his work. He had to move to the second shift, and that left me counting the hours till he came home.

When the children were still home, I used to wonder what it would be like to have the house all to myself. Now I found it was not much fun. Bruce could watch whatever he wanted on TV, flipping channels to his heart's content. I just wanted him nearby.

As I began to look at my husband with new eyes, I realized Bruce deserved someone who would serve him, someone who would love him the way he loved me.

He is so good, so gentle, so loving, and so kind. He has all the fruits of the Spirit. He is wonderful, I mused. Then I realized, *I love him.*

I could not believe it. After close to forty years of marriage, I fell in love with my husband.

Everything was different after that. I could not wait for him to come home. I told him I loved him all the time. It wasn't hard at all. I was no longer embarrassed if he kissed me in public. I looked forward to his kisses. We took neighborhood walks, holding hands. It felt good to want to be near him.

It was so much fun loving my husband, hearing his voice, seeing his smile, hearing him laugh. If only I were not such a burden, he really could do so much better.

The pain was bad, even severe at times. Watching my husband hurt for me was worse. That's when he prayed I would die.

I was in my green recliner. Bruce had brought me my pain pill. He watched me bend my head and cover my face in defeat. It was useless to even try to hold the glass of water or reach for the pill.

He got on his knees, grabbed my hand, and prayed, "Father, if it is your will, take Laquita home so she does not have to suffer."

His tears splashed on my arm as I felt his whole body shake.

He does not love me, I thought with surprise. Then, in my heart, I knew he was praying this because he *did* love me. He loved me enough to give me back to God if it was God's will.

He did not want me to die because I was a burden. He was suffering because I was suffering. He did not want me to suffer if God had a better plan. He had done everything he could — even pray the prayer he did not want to pray.

I know how hard it was for him to pray that prayer. I never felt so loved in all my life. I never loved my husband as much as I did then.

God said no to Bruce's prayer. In time, my doctors found the medicine that has kept my illness under control. I can now function and serve my husband and let him serve me without feeling guilty.

Falling in love with my husband changed

my life. It was a gift I was afraid to receive. Falling in love is a risk well worth taking. I am no longer in that bondage of fear. I am free to love.

— *Laquita Havens*

Sometimes, like Laquita, it's hard for us to believe that someone else really cares. It's hard for us to rest in the assurance that this love is true — especially if we feel we are not giving as well in return.

And when we don't trust a person's love for us, we tend not to love in return. We tend to hold back, afraid of giving. It's like having a beautiful swimming pool in your yard, but on a steaming summer day not enjoying the pool for fear that you might drown.

While none of us longs for challenges, at times it takes the fires of life's trials to help us realize that another person's love is as pure, strong, and reliable as gold.

When we're willing to trust another's love, we can take the risk to be authentic. As we step out and trust another, we can swim in the cool waters of love, enjoying the refreshment and pure fun.

Have you only been putting your foot in the pool? Let go and jump in. The water's fine!

THE BATTLE OF THE DISHWASHER

Before getting married, my husband and I went through premarital counseling. We touched on many subjects that spark arguments between a husband and wife: money, family, beliefs, goals, physical intimacy, etc. But nothing in those counseling sessions could have prepared me for the primary cause of our worst battles the first few years of marriage.

We fought over how to load the dishwasher.

My husband was reared with definite rules on how a dishwasher should be loaded, and each rule had a practical reason behind it. Plastic almost never goes in the bottom rack, lest it become warped. Forks should only go with other forks in the silverware basket, knives with knives, teaspoons with teaspoons, and soup spoons with soup spoons. If you do this, unloading is a simple matter of grabbing a handful and putting them away at once without having to sort through utensils.

Other rules come into play, but these will give you the general idea.

I grew up with basic guidelines that followed common sense (load the forks and knives point down to avoid stabbing yourself when unloading), but in the face of all of my husband's pragmatic rules, I rebelled. Why should I have to do it *his* way? My family managed to have clean dishes for years without following all those rules!

As petty as it was, I would thwart his rules where possible, just to do it my way — and to get under his skin, I'm embarrassed to confess. I loaded the dishwasher the way *I* wanted — he said he was attracted to me for my independence, right? Then I fumed as he came along behind me and rearranged items according to his preferences.

As is so often the case in marriage, our fights about the dishwasher escalated into bigger issues. I would get self-righteous and declare that no future child of ours should feel her best was not good enough. How would a small family member feel when Daddy came along behind them and "corrected" how they loaded their dishes?

I was sure our children would feel crushed and never feel satisfied with anything they did. "We live under grace, not under the *law!*" I announced more than once, sure that even the Bible would agree with me.

My husband insisted that the rules he followed were not arbitrary; they were in place for good reasons. Did I *want* our plastic dishes to be warped? Would I reject an idea out of stubbornness, even if it was best? He felt pride was an issue I needed to deal with — especially if it meant I was rejecting the *right* way to do things!

Somehow about the second or third year of marriage we agreed to live and let live. He would load dishes as he saw fit, and I would load them as I wanted. We agreed not to redo or "correct" the other's loading style, and we tried to extend more grace for each other — and have more humility.

He had a tough time overcoming decades of habit. I realized this the day I overheard him on a support call of sorts with one of his sisters. They coached each other about how it was okay, even if it was hard, to put teaspoons and soup spoons into the same divider in the silverware basket.

They had to talk each other into allowing a rule to be broken; it offended their natural inclinations! I think setting aside any loading rules must have been like hearing fingernails on a chalkboard for him.

I tried to recognize that what I considered small things actually required sacrifice on his part — and that he chose to make that sacrifice out of love for me.

Now I work to conform to his comfort level where possible, purely as a way of loving him. No, I see no need for all plastic to be in the upper rack, but does it cost me anything but pride to honor him in such a small way? He may appreciate my independence, but he appreciates it more when I choose to set aside my way to show my love for him instead of having to prove I'm right.

Early in our marriage we decided that aside from our individual relationship with God, no aspect of our selves, whether habits, choices, or personal preferences, was off-limits to change. I don't know if we made that decision by design or pure grace, but I suspect we stumbled into grace.

I don't want to hold any aspect of my life over my husband's head, saying it is more important to me than he is. If a choice I make pulls me away from a unified marriage rather than toward it, I need to recognize it and change. I am learning that marriage is more about surrendering than fighting to maintain self.

We still have our faults, and we are as different as we always were! It bothers me to this day that he does not anchor light pieces down in the dishwasher with heavier pieces so they will not flip over and fill with water during the wash cycle.

He still gets frustrated by the way I load glasses over the posts in a rack rather than between the upright posts. It still takes conscious self-control at times to prevent "fixing" how the other person has loaded dishes so they are loaded as we each prefer them.

We had a rather amusing revisit to all our battles just a few years ago. My in-laws were in town and stayed with my parents. One of those days, my husband and I were in my parents' family room. From the kitchen, we overheard the same debates we had our first year of marriage: My dad had loaded the dishwasher, and my mother-in-law, loading her breakfast dishes, came along behind him and reloaded all the dishes the way they "should" have been loaded. She explained why she was changing things around.

My dad responded much as I had! Their debate ended much quicker since they were not married. We tried to stifle our laughter, understanding better why our battles had been so long and heated. We were also very thankful that we had reached a point that we *could* laugh rather than cringe!

We learned that a wholehearted relationship is not possible unless each person is committed to choosing love first. This doesn't just mean in the big areas of work, finances, family, and such, but also in the seemingly inconsequential things. We can ask, *Am I willing to set aside my pride for a very specific moment in time and choose to extend love and grace? In every confrontation, in every fight over whose way is right, will I choose love or will I choose pride?*

With regard to choices, in baby steps over days, weeks, and months that gradually turn into years, we are learning to choose *us* rather than me — even in something so small, so petty, as loading the dishwasher.

— *Susan Stanley*

Have you ever found yourself in a heated battle with a friend or loved one about something that's actually rather silly? So many times we get all upset over differences of opinion or things that really aren't important. But how these matters grow! Before long, our relationships are lying in a crumpled heap over which way the toilet paper should hang, or who treated whom the last time we went out for dinner together.

When little conflicts threaten to rip at the fabric of your relationship, one question to ask is: Does it really matter?

Is the issue we're arguing about more important than the relationship itself?

If we're holding on to our "right" to be right, we should just give in. If we're holding on to a silly argument out of pride, we should just give in. We don't lose when we graciously concede.

When it comes to fighting in a relationship, choose your battles wisely. Only use the emotional energy on things that really matter. And you might be surprised at how few things in life are really worth a fight.

THE WEATHER
KITTEN

I stared in wonder at the glass shelf filled with knickknacks. In my small town, the five-and-dime store was about the only place for a young girl to shop. The coins I'd saved bit into my palm through a cloth handkerchief.

This is it! I thought as my eyes landed on the perfect gift for my mother. I could almost see the delight on her face when she opened my present on her birthday. Excitement raced through me as I pointed to the small ceramic kitten so the storeowner could take it down.

The clerk handed me the off-white figurine, and I opened the printed tag tied around its neck. It read: The Weather Kitten. The rough surface of the small animal chafed against my hand as I read how the figure was intended to reflect the weather outside. On days when snow was expected, the kitten's coat would turn gray. Rain changed the finish to blue, and sunshine would be shown in pure white.

Each weather condition was listed with the color to look for, so you would know how to dress before you walked out the door. I smiled with delight as I paid the white-haired gentleman for my gift.

On my mother's birthday, I couldn't sit still as I waited for her to open my package. I knew that while Mother stood at the sink washing dishes or preparing meals, she often looked out the window and commented on the weather, surmising what we could expect if we went outside.

Mom loved to listen to the news to see what the weatherman would predict for the next day. I knew she'd be excited to have this kitten help her know what was ahead. I didn't stop to consider that she didn't care that much for cats. After all, I loved them enough for both of us, and this blue-eyed cutie was sure to charm.

When Mom pulled the kitten from the box, I edged forward, eager to show her all the ways this gift would be beneficial. We read the tag together, and she placed the ceramic cat on the windowsill where we could both check it each day to see what color the pebbled surface would show. Because it was December and we lived in a colder climate, I knew we would see much more gray and blue than white.

Every day as Mom washed the dishes and I helped, I covertly glanced at the little figure. We had rain. We had snow. We had sunshine. Through it all, the kitten remained off-white, the same as when I'd first spotted it in the store. It refused to change color as promised on the tag.

Mom must have noticed my disappointment. I had saved my allowance to buy something special for her birthday. I felt like I had wasted that money. The kitten was cute but didn't foretell the weather. I wondered if Mom was also disappointed in me because I gave her a gift that didn't work.

"Why don't we move this to a higher shelf on the window," Mom said. "Perhaps the sill is too low for the change to occur. The window frame might be blocking the light."

Day after day my mother would comment about the small cat. "Don't you think there's more blue in the coat today?" or "I'm sure this is a darker gray than yesterday. We must be getting ready to have snow."

I would glance outside at the low, heavy clouds and realize that even I could tell everyone it would snow.

Years passed. I grew up, married, and left

home. Dad and Mom moved to a different house. When I visited their new home, I was amazed to see the small weather kitten on a shelf next to the kitchen window, still looking outside waiting for sun, snow, or rain. Touched that my mother would keep a useless gift, I began to ponder the lessons my mother taught me through the experience.

Mom didn't love that kitten, she loved me. She loved that I had spent my meager allowance to buy her something I thought she would like. Instead of being disgusted over a gift that was worthless, she saw the worth in the giver's intent. I have never forgotten that lesson, even though she instilled by example, not with words.

My mother also taught me to consider other people. I think of all the people in her life. She cares enough to learn small details about them, which she turns into little gestures of love that mean so much. Many times she takes a piece of pie to someone in a nursing home because she remembers it is his favorite dessert. Mom makes homemade jams and recalls who likes which fruit so she can give them a jar. Because of her example, I've learned to listen to what others say about themselves. I know which people like certain foods or colors, and I try to incorporate that into a gift for them.

I learned that love is a matter of how you view life. When I looked at that knickknack, I saw failure and disappointment. When my mother looked at the same gift, she saw success because I'd chosen the kitten especially for her. To her, the figurine's failure to fulfill its purpose had no bearing on its value. The only difference between my mother and me was our outlook. Instead of viewing the negative, she saw the positive.

Mom showed me that love doesn't give up. We had many difficult years; times when I wasn't there for her, or did things that hurt her. Yet she didn't throw away that kitten. She kept it in a prominent place, even though there must have been pain with the memories it evoked. She still kept hoping our relationship would mend. When it did, she didn't flaunt her ability to love, but continued loving as she always had.

Over the years, I've received my own share of gifts that were not what they were touted to be. I have several displayed in prominent places. Each time I look at them — especially my children's gifts — I think of the giver, and how that person thought of me when they chose that gift. I often recall a small kitten sitting on a windowsill far from me, and the final lesson: Love teaches others how to love — and I have to smile. From mother to daughter to grandchild, a worthless weather kitten becomes the most precious gift of all.

— *Nancy J. Farrier*

What a wonderful lesson for all of us: that love is a perspective. Sometimes people disappoint us by what they do or say. But what a great reminder to look beyond the outward appearances to the intent of the heart! When we focus on the heart, it's not hard to overlook another person's mistakes and failings. As one of the wise men of the Bible, Peter, pointed out, "Love covers a multitude of sins" (1 Peter 4:8).

And when we're the giver who's afraid we've disappointed someone we care about, let's remember not to underestimate the power of love. People who truly care do so because of who we are — not because of what we can do for them, or give to them, or be for them. Instead, those who love us see us with their hearts . . . hearts that look behind actuality to our motivations.

Say Good-bye to Your Mistress

"You know I love you, right?" he said with a sideways glance as he walked back into the apartment with a laundry basket full of warm, clean clothes. A smile crossed his lips as he studied my expression.

"Really? Wow."

Inside I was leaping with joy. But on the outside, these two simple words became my response to the pronouncement I'd been longing to hear for months. Maybe I was just stunned at the nonchalant way he stated his feelings. I'm sure my expression was comical — pure astonishment layered with complete relief.

We had met months earlier, at a workplace celebration just days before the Christmas holiday. He asked me out on a date. Dinner and a movie: safe, predictable, and surprisingly fun. We settled on a time for him to pick me up, and we parted ways, one rung above strangers on the relational ladder.

That next night we tromped through freshly fallen snow in the parking lot as we hurried into the warm hallways of the movie theater. When we settled into our seats, munching popcorn and waiting for the previews to roll, my man of little words pronounced a truth I wouldn't fully comprehend for years to come: "The army is my mistress."

Yeah, right, I thought. *What kind of comment is that? Why would he tell me that on a first date?*

I brushed it off but would have been wiser to heed the warning.

His reserved demeanor and polite banter were charming, but I didn't expect this to amount to a lasting relationship — unless he opened up a bit more. My aptitude for relationships was limited to what I heard and saw. I still had a lot to learn about love.

Months after that first date, when he carried his words of love with a laundry basket, our lifelong love affair finally began. Sure, we'd been getting to know each other, and yes, we liked to hang out together. But I believe true love begins when the secret longings of our heart spill out into our lives. His words connected with my soul. Until that moment I'd been holding back my emotions. Now my heart was pressing on, full steam ahead, and ready to consider a life committed to this man.

We grew in our love, even though that looming mistress was always sneaking phone calls and nighttime visits. She (the army) was always calling. An urgent meeting here, a need to travel there, and he was off with very little explanation.

Insecurities plagued me as I wondered what he was thinking or how ready he was to share his life with me. I wasn't sure I wanted to share his attention with anyone — especially with what I considered a job instead of the *adventure* the television commercials described the army to be.

We continued to date. We toured the local sights and talked about our interests and general details of our lives. In the back of my mind I explored many hidden worries. *Can I love someone who seems to have such an emotional wall built between us? Will he ever openly express how he feels? Can I function in a relationship with someone so different from me? Will I have enough patience for long work hours and frequent separations?*

On our wedding day, I saw him standing there in his dress blues and the reality of military life crashed in on me. It was true. The army was the 24/7 focus of a mind committed to protecting our freedom.

Anything, even family, would have to take a backseat.

The love we shared only hit the number two slot on the top ten list of his life. I had to learn to share his love with duty, country, and freedom. Nothing would have kept me from falling in love with this man, and my sense of patriotism grew as I learned what compelled him to serve and experience the life of those who support our country.

While I wouldn't have changed a thing about his commitment to his country, I had to change my expectations. I was faced with the challenge of having to mature in how I handled relationships.

Through the next thirteen years of active military duty, our love weathered the storms of late night office hours, deployments, training exercises, and community support. I learned to love through the times when he was half a world away, or when his dinner grew cold awaiting his arrival. I juggled the roles of being the dad, the mom, the nurse when our son was sick, and the playmate while Daddy was serving our country.

We experienced times apart with limited conversation before the age of the Internet and the cell phone. I was learning how to love beyond communication barriers in so many ways! Some years this life's challenges brought such a feeling of distance in our home that I imagine we both prayed we'd find the strength to build intimacy in our marriage again. In the midst of deployments and hectic schedules, introverted men like mine tend to find little time to reinforce the walls of the home front through words.

We maneuvered through our relationship with the understanding that we loved and were loved — no matter the circumstances or trials we faced. I would survive every moment of insecurity and doubt if I recognized that his love was not limited to his ability to express it verbally. I'd be fine if I'd learn to love a man of few words.

What kept my love strong? My heart held on because of that simple afternoon affirmation. On countless days the image of my mate holding a basket in one hand and my heart in the other reminded me that we had a spark that had been fanned into flames. Underneath our daily lives was a love that would withstand any silence or separation.

Our relationship was built on trust, love, and yes, even a few words. Over time I learned to love beyond mere sight and sound.

My husband's expressions of love are found in a variety of ways — through integrity, honesty, service, and support. The more I understand how he shows devotion, the more I'm able to rest in the peace of knowing that I am loved.

At the end of twenty-four years, he said good-bye to his mistress. He retired, and in the blink of an eye, our family climbed to the top of his list. We were finally allowed to be the number one focus in his life, the prime target of love and priority. After years of figuring out how to survive as the shared love of a wonderful man's life, I was blessed with the realization that nothing could capture my husband's interest more than his family.

Our love still grows stronger. I wouldn't have traded a thing. I wouldn't have missed out on a second of military life. I wouldn't have wanted anyone else with whom to share my life.

But the in-between years have given me a glimpse into learning to love someone who approaches relationships far differently than I've ever experienced. After all, a man of little words is a complex challenge for any woman who wears her heart on her sleeve. And you know what? It's okay. I know he loves me.

— *Jennifer Devlin*

In an insecure world, it's not uncommon for

us to want to have "proof" or reassurance that someone we care about returns our feelings of affection. Our imaginations interpret silence, distraction, and preoccupation as signs that the love is fading.

That's one of the reasons it's so important to understand the love language of a person we care about. Some people just show their affection in a different way than we do. And chances are, if we're in a friendship or a love relationship with a "strong, silent type" we're not going to hear or see frequent, obvious displays of affection.

We just have to trust that someone who says he loves us actually does even though he doesn't frequently reaffirm that commitment. Instead of assuming the worst, we have to expect the best. Like Jennifer, we have to learn that stable, mature love is deeper than emotional words and displays of affection. The words and touches are nice, sure, but they're not everyone's way of expressing love. The key is to change our expectations to something that is reasonably within our loved one's personality.

The 50/50 Proposition

As I looked at my husband, I suddenly realized this was it: Our marriage had hit rock bottom.

Rock bottom came when the oldest of our five children was a teenager. We had recently lost our house to fire, and with no insurance we found ourselves transplanted from our dream home in the forest to a crowded two-bedroom house in the middle of town. The crisis alone was enough to make or break a marriage, but the adjustment from country to city living nearly did us in.

When I opened my front door to holler for the children to come in for lunch, the echo resounded for blocks. I quickly learned that it takes less volume to yell down a city street than it does across twenty acres.

The children had their own problems. Coming from the country, they were tagged with names such as *goat ropers* and *hillbillies*. Our oldest son found a different way home from school every day to avoid the inevitable fistfight. Our youngest son dealt with the changes by turning into a whiner.

Yet through it all, my husband, Cat, faced the biggest adjustment. The company he worked for went out of business. He found himself in the unemployment line facing day after day of rejection.

If I had been wise, I would have helped him through that rejection, but instead I added to it.

I didn't feel Cat was reaching out to the kids enough. He didn't understand their problems. He didn't understand mine. How could I feed a family of seven with so little money? And we had no alone time. The boys had one bedroom, the girls the other, while Cat and I slept on a hide-a-bed in the living room. So every argument, and there were plenty of them, involved the entire family.

On this particular day, my rock-bottom day, I resorted to tears while my husband stood over me and shared his views that our boys would have to fight their own battles. Cat's opinion came after I stepped between my oldest son and a neighborhood bully. "You have to stay out of the middle of it," Cat said.

I looked up at him ready to plead my case.

Instead, I caught my breath at the shock of anger in his eyes. Where had the love gone? The concern? What had happened to the romance?

Some people talk about how in a moment of facing death their lives flash before them. That's what happened to me as I faced the death of our love. The long-ago months of courtship rolled before me like a newsreel running in my mind. When did Cat stop bringing me flowers? When was the last time he had taken me on a date? When was the last time he had invited me *anywhere?*

Suddenly, I had to get out. I ran through the door and jumped in my car, peeling rubber in the street. I could barely see for the tears. Without a plan, I drove. Who could I turn to? Who would understand? Cat was my best friend. If I couldn't turn to him —

That was the moment I realized I couldn't live without Cat and I couldn't live with him. *Ouch!*

I ended up on a dirt road overlooking the wild and scenic Rogue River. I planned to hurl myself into the raging water churning over Gold Ray Dam, but I lost my nerve. Determined not to let fear stop me the second time, I drove farther down the river, below the dam, and slammed the car to a stop.

I jumped out and started wading into the water. The Rogue River was famous for carrying people away. It claimed several victims every year. I figured I would just walk out until it carried me away, but this was not to be my day. I walked across the river, turned around, and came back.

It must have been the only section that was slow and wide enough to do so. Or perhaps it was God performing a miracle like He did with the Red Sea in the Old Testament. I returned to the car, wet and cold, but still very much alive. Like others saved from the jaws of death, I sat there and bawled, pleading with God to help me.

I didn't hear an audible voice from heaven, but a slow awareness washed over me until I realized I had a lot to be thankful for. I had a husband who treated me with kindness most of the time. He was trustworthy and faithful, diligent in providing for our family, and a strong leader. Perhaps unrealistic expectations had been hiding the truth from me.

I returned home. Cat was out in the garage and didn't see me change into dry clothes. I never said a word about where I had been.

My biggest challenge stood before me. For the first time in our marriage, I had walked out on my husband. He was hurt and showed it by becoming a rock wall. My first tendency was to run away, head back to the river. Instead, I tried to touch Cat, but nothing softened. His muscles were hard and stiff.

I felt as if I had lost everything, but in truth, I still had something left to give, so I gave it: I prepared a simple meal for my family.

Sure, I felt like a workhorse. I wondered if preparing meals and cleaning house was all my husband wanted of me. If so, he could hire a housekeeper and a cook and do just fine.

Normally I would have gone on with such thoughts, but this time I decided to stop them. As I dished up mashed potatoes, I replaced my negative thoughts with good ones. These weren't just Pollyanna thoughts. They were true thoughts. My husband was kind. He was a hard worker. There was a time, though it seemed very long ago, that he liked to laugh and have fun. He taught the boys how to fish and ride bikes. He said the words "I love you" often. That alone was a treasure for which most women would pay money. He snored. . . .

I dropped my fork and laughed.

My family all stopped eating and looked

at me. I just shook my head. JayJay, our oldest son, relaxed and started telling a joke.

I wished I could share my joke, but I didn't think my family could quite understand. My husband snored when he slept at night. How funny was that? Most women would have to buy earplugs or something, but I slept best when Cat's snores filled the silence. Surely that was proof of our long-standing love.

I reached out and touched my husband's hand. This time, Cat's fingers folded around mine, and I saw the love in his eyes that had been there all along. I also saw the hurt that I had misread as hate. Was it my expectations of seeing my own needs met that had kept me from realizing the truth?

Give more and take less. Expect less.

The realization from the river of adjusting my expectations came back to me, and it is with me to this day. Like an answer to a prayer from a foxhole, it was God's answer to me. This insight not only colors the relationship between my husband and me but it also colors all my other relationships. I've gained friendships that I would have been afraid to start, friendships where I receive very little in the way of someone calling or thinking of me, but friendships that have added depth and meaning to my life. Some people can never reach out for fear of rejection, but these same people accept love with delight and charm.

Expecting less, I am more thankful. Giving more, I receive more.

I have discovered romance — one that spurs storybooks and fairy tales — and I have found it in my own marriage. Cat is my shining knight, and I will forever be his beautiful princess no matter what time and age do to our bodies. Arguments are shorter lived than they used to be and come less often. I seldom complain about the raised toilet seat or even about the piece of plywood covering the dry rot of our kitchen floor. Toilet seats and kitchen floors come and go, but relationships last forever.

I've regretted words spoken in haste — pain caused needlessly when I've lashed out in hurt. Sometimes it's difficult to squash my expectations as I sit on the edge of the bed and wish my husband would come to me. But I have never once regretted laying down those expectations and giving more of myself by reaching out in love.

I've always heard that marriage is a 50/50 deal — each partner gives 50 percent and the other meets them halfway. Yet after nearly forty years of marriage to a man I can't get enough of, to a man I love more every day, I can say with resounding certainty that marriage is not a 50/50 deal. It takes 100 percent commitment from both partners.

This 100 percent commitment has brought me more and longer-lasting joy than any 50/50 deal could ever offer.

— *Sandy Cathcart*

One of the biggest fallacies about successful relationships is that they're a 50/50 proposition. As Sandy found, for the ideal marriage each person in a relationship has to give 100 percent. But in order for us to know peace and fulfillment we have to give that 100 percent whether the other person is giving 100 percent, or only 10 percent. When we focus on where we have fallen short and work on that, we often see the other's percentage go up.

It's one of those dichotomies of life: The more we give of ourselves, the more we receive. The less we expect from others, the more we get.

Sometimes this doesn't seem fair, and it certainly doesn't seem to make sense. But it's one of the keys to a living, growing relationship. This is one of the great secrets for making a friendship and a love affair with our spouse work.

FOR RICHER OR POORER

The marriage vows were easy: "For better or for worse, for richer or poorer, in sickness and in health, to love and to cherish."

For better or for worse? That was no problem. We loved each other, and life could only get better once we were married.

For richer or poorer? Well, we knew we'd both be poorer for many years. We were buying a house, and to be honest, we couldn't afford it.

But *in sickness and in health?* When you're in your twenties, sickness means nothing more than the occasional cold or tummy bug. We could manage those. We'd coped with that sort of thing ever since we were born.

Then suddenly after thirty-seven years of a great marriage of loving and cherishing, Liz was diagnosed with Alzheimer's disease. And that really *is* a sickness.

No way was I going to let Liz go into a

care facility. I could manage. And for three years I *did* manage. At first it was fairly easy. The medication worked, and Liz's memory score rose to the point where she believed she was better. But of course nothing in life is that easy.

In August her memory became worse again, and she started to have behavioral problems. Hey, not to worry, we'd promised that we'd be there for each other in sickness and in health. I'd see it through to the end.

The changes were slow but steady. It was a bit like watching weeds grow in the backyard. Things happen so slowly you hardly notice — until you get back from a long vacation. That's when you realize how much the plants have changed.

But I didn't get that break, so I hardly noticed how badly Liz's condition was worsening.

Friends from church rallied round. They were great. A good friend warned me that I had to look after myself, but I was doing fine — apart from the chest and stomach pains that were nothing more than indigestion brought on by a little bit of stress. Not that the antacid did much good.

The local health authority sent a helper to give me a break during the day. As far as Liz was concerned the woman was unwelcome. So was the next one, and the next. Liz thought they had moved in with us, and she was afraid to go to bed at night in case they were in the room with us. And I couldn't go out and leave Liz with one of the helpers anyway in case she became too agitated, so the stress continued. And so did the love. In fact, looking back, I can see that our love was actually strengthened.

The more Liz's condition worsened, the more my love for her grew. We'd always been a very loving couple, but this seemed like an extra special love, and she was able to return it with hugs and kisses. But it didn't solve the stomach pains.

One morning in March, I woke up with a crushing pain in my chest. It couldn't possibly be my heart, I reasoned, and anyway I had no pain in my left arm. Besides, I had to look after Liz.

Liz managed to get some antacid, and this seemed to fix things. The pain didn't return, and four days later I felt brave enough to look up the symptoms of a heart attack on the Internet.

It seemed that a heart attack could start with stomach pains. Well, maybe it could, but I definitely hadn't had a heart attack. I knew that for sure.

Well, not quite for sure. On Monday

morning I was seeing my doctor for a checkup, just to be on the safe side. He immediately transferred me to the local hospital for a checkup, also just to be on the safe side.

Liz had to go with me. I couldn't arrange for anyone to look after her until the afternoon, so she sat by my side, wandering off from time to time as she became bored.

The hospital staff knew she had Alzheimer's, but I was the patient and they wouldn't take responsibility for her. So each time she went out of sight I had to get up to bring her back. I wasn't wired up yet, so it was easy enough.

Fortunately, my daughter was able to come from her work and take Liz home before lunch. A friend from church who had been a nurse checked on Liz during the afternoon. By then I was wired and tubed up and given blood tests. Yes, I'd had a heart attack.

"Will I be going home today?" I asked naïvely. "My wife needs me."

The family brought Liz to see me in the hospital the next day. Things were going well at home, or so they told me. They probably didn't want to add to my stress.

The tests showed that I had two blocked

arteries that could probably be fixed with stents.

I had to stay in the hospital, and this could be a matter of weeks. I knew that Liz wouldn't understand what was going on, even if the family told her.

The next Sunday was Easter — the first Easter we'd not gone to church together. I was taken to the hospital chapel in a wheelchair, and after the service the chaplain asked me what was wrong.

I started to tell her about Liz, and the tears came. I couldn't speak. I'm sure the rest of those present thought I was crying because I'd been given the devastating diagnosis. Not that I cared what they thought. My tears were for Liz.

After ten days, the family was no longer able to cope. Liz had to go into temporary care. She had been brought to see me several times, and knew I was no longer at home. Our oldest son bravely volunteered to take his mom to a specialist care unit, and I'm sure there were tears there as well.

The trauma of going into care was not as devastating for Liz as I had feared. She settled within forty-eight hours, and I phoned her a few times and said I'd be seeing her soon.

Nearly four weeks passed before I could

leave the hospital, and this turned out to be a great blessing. Liz seemed to accept that we were parted, and the family could visit her without her crying when they left. The expert assessment on Liz was that she needed to stay in full-time care. So now I had to find a permanent care home for her.

The local health authority gave me a list of approved homes, and I quickly found one that seemed fine. I took some of her favorite pictures and ornaments to decorate her room in her new home and was in the room when she arrived.

Yes, there were tears, but there were hugs and kisses too. Liz never asked to come home. One day she asked me if we had a home somewhere, and I said, "No, not at the moment."

We didn't have a home. I lived in the house that had once been our home, determined to make the best of my life from then on.

Once Liz had settled in, I took her to the local church every Sunday. I didn't want to go to the church where we had first met and had worshiped ever since. I wanted Liz to think that she was living a new life, without remembering the past.

As Liz's condition worsened she had to be moved again, this time to a secure nursing home. The pictures and ornaments were there when she arrived. And so was I. She settled in again remarkably quickly, and is still holding on.

In sickness and in health? Maybe deep down, all those years ago, I thought that one of us might get a serious illness later in life. But that was far in the future. I'm glad the prospect of long-term ill health never worried either of us, because when it happened we had the strength to cope with it.

For richer or poorer? The house was eventually paid for, and things got easier financially for us as a family. But richer? Forget the money. Surely, the richness is the extra capacity we both discovered for love. The love was always there, but in the time of suffering it became greater and even more important.

I think back to our wedding in the little country church in the village where Liz was raised. We both said "I do."

Knowing what I know now, would I say it again? Yes I would, without a single doubt. We're both much richer for having said it.

— *Chris Wright*

A wise mentor once said, "We often wish we knew God's plan for our lives. But we can be glad God doesn't lay out the direction of our whole lives for us to see — if He did, we'd probably run scared."

Likewise, it's probably good that when we begin a relationship, we never know where it will lead. If we knew ours would be one of those relationships, like Chris's, that would face pain and challenge, we would probably hesitate! And in doing so, we'd probably also miss out on some of the greatest joys in our lives.

While no relationship is guaranteed a pain-free future, as Chris learned, love is still worth it.

And how does love weather the storms of life? A firm foundation helps. One of the keys is to build strength and nurture love during the sunny, warm days of camaraderie . . . to focus on and deepen the closeness day by day. Then if the storms hit, we can survive them because our relationship is already firmly planted and rooted in deep soil.

Take time today to nurture your relationships.

THE PRICE IS WORTH IT

The marriage was disastrous. The divorce was dreadful. The custody battle was devastating — can love grow out of such calamity?

I married for all the wrong reasons. He was six feet two, eyes of blue, and the body of a Greek god.

Twenty-five years and three children later, I walked away from an abusive man who promptly filed for custody of our ten-year-old daughter. Unknown to me at the time, the judge was my ex-husband's new wife's friend who, without investigation, gave custody to my ex-husband. He hid my letters to her, changed and unlisted his phone number, and placed her in a private school where I couldn't see her.

Once he left my daughter and her stepsister alone for three days with no adult supervision. On the very night my ex-husband and his wife returned, an intruder attempted to rape her. Instances like this kept me anguished, for I knew my daughter was not safe.

I spent more than two years and thousands of dollars fighting for her. I was filled with rage and hatred for this man. I prayed he would die — a long, painful death. When I heard his fourth wife was divorcing him, I again fought for my daughter. My ex-husband and I were both investigated. I received a good report; he was pronounced a sociopath.

I received immediate custody. But how was I to handle it? Should I deny him visitation? Hide her in another state? Hire a hit man? (No, not a serious consideration, but there were days!)

Common sense told me that my rage would give him control of the rest of my life. So I chose to act out of my will and not my emotions. Still strongly resenting him, I gave him my daughter's address and phone number, as well as the name of the school she would attend. When he came to visit her, we invited him to join us for dinner. And I sometimes considered sprinkling arsenic in his coffee. I never thought I could ever have loving feelings toward this man. What's more, I didn't want to feel love for him. He didn't deserve it!

Then I was diagnosed with a brain tumor and I was not expected to live. When I did recover, I realized for the first time that we all have a date with death, and it can happen any time. Did I want to die hating my children's father?

Again, I made a choice. Although my feelings toward him were hostile, I chose to treat him like a loved relative instead.

When my daughter graduated, we included him in the festivities. When she was chosen Louisiana Orange Queen, we insisted that she invite him to escort her in all her activities. We freed her to fly to see him anytime she wanted to. Eventually my family began to thaw and he warmed just a little. We were still afraid of him, never knowing when he might become threatening, but we could be civil.

I believe my serious illness helped him realize that life is fragile and he needed to mend some fences. Meanwhile I concentrated on showing him kindness, even though I still battled the demons of vengeance and anger. *It isn't fair,* I thought, and I tended to listen to the whiny voice of self-pity. *Why me?*

Hadn't he refused to let me pursue my hobbies? Hadn't he been unfaithful too often to count? Hadn't he just divorced his fourth wife? Why should I feel compassion? Hadn't I given him the best twenty-five years of my life, forgiven him, and tried to save our marriage? Wasn't this enough?

Evidently not, for when I filled my mind with negative thoughts, I lost my sense of well-being. So again, I would choose to perform a kind act.

When our oldest daughter married, she and I sang "Edelweiss," the favorite song of his deceased German parents. I think I saw a tear in his eye as we noted his parents' absence from their favorite grandchild's wedding.

I knew he had committed many evil acts and that his health was rapidly failing. I hoped he would mend his relationships with his brother, his children, and other family and friends before it was too late.

The Christmas before he died, he called me aside and asked if I ever watched a certain television evangelist who lost most of his ministry when he committed adultery.

"Don't you think he should be forgiven?" he asked.

"Of course," I answered, trembling as usual when I had to confront him.

"Don't you think he is a lonely old man whom nobody cares about? He knows he has ruined many lives. Maybe if he could experience life over again, he would do it differently."

I agreed that this was a possibility. It took me a bit to realize that in his roundabout way, he was seeking my forgiveness.

I talked to him one last time before he died. He called to invite me to watch another Christian speaker on TV, saying the young minister had changed his life. His tone sounded humble.

When I received the call that he was gone, I was surprised to feel that I had lost a loved one. Somewhere in my journey toward wholeness, my hateful feelings toward him had changed and I wanted him to find peace and joy. I no longer wished he'd get payback for his actions. Over time I'd realized that he had suffered the consequences of all his acts of selfishness. He had lived with a mean spirit and driven away all those who loved him, and he died alone. For this I grieved. Yes, I grieved for the man he could have been while I rejoiced to see a glimpse of the man he was becoming in the months before his death.

I do not know what part I played in his coming to terms with his life. But I do know that he was like sandpaper in my life. From him, I learned to choose to make a sacrifice of love. And sacrifice hurts. In order to love unconditionally, a person must refuse to hate or to seek revenge. A little of yourself must die when you choose to love the one who trampled you in the dust and injured you.

This kind of love exacts a price, but refusing to love costs so much more.

— *Jacquelyn Sandifer Strange*

By its very nature, a sacrifice is painful. It means giving up something. If it didn't hurt or call for uncomfortable giving, it wouldn't be called a sacrifice.

It's not all that difficult to make sacrifices for someone with whom we are "in love." When a relationship is good, we can sacrifice without regret . . . and the pain of giving seems negligible.

But as Jacquelyn points out, when love is a difficult choice — when it includes forgiving and deciding to love "in spite of" — it calls for a great deal of sacrifice. And that hurts. It calls for us to let little portions of ourselves die.

As we put our hatred and desires for revenge to death and choose to love, sometimes this death brings a new life to the person we choose to love. But regardless of that, by choosing to love, we choose to shed pain and find more abundant lives ourselves.

Pulling Weeds on Blossom Trail

"Who's pulling out the wildflowers in our garden?" I asked.

"Oh, that must be Judy. She said our weeds were encroaching on her property," my husband replied with a grin.

"How would she like it if I traipsed across her backyard and cut down her trees that are hanging over our fence?" I retorted.

"C'mon, honey, Judy means well. She just likes to have things *her* way," my husband explained.

"But don't you think she should have called first to let us know that she was upset with our wildflower patch?" I asked.

Mark shrugged and finished reading the Sunday paper. He didn't seem concerned. After all, it wasn't the first time Judy had taken matters into her own hands when things weren't exactly perfect in the neighborhood.

We had recently moved into the development, which was a quiet community with a blend of working couples, young families, and retirees.

It was our oasis!

In fact, after twenty-seven moves in thirty-two years, we could finally call it home. Our townhouse was ideal. We bought the model home with a gorgeous view of the common property. We enjoyed an unobstructed view of spectacular sunsets from our patio, access to walking trails right at our doorstep, and friendly neighbors at every turn — except our next-door neighbor on Blossom Trail.

Since our townhouse was in the middle of the row of three, we were sensitive to making too much noise. But when a football game came on and my three guys watched the Giants face the Eagles, their shouts, groans, and roars rivaled any crowd in the bleachers. At those times, I knew Judy would call and tell us to turn down the volume.

It happened at the beginning of the third quarter after the Giants had scored a touchdown and the guys let out a "HOORAH!" Then — just as predictably as the Philadelphia Eagles missed the interception — the phone rang.

"You answer it this time," my husband

directed. "Tell Judy we'll turn the volume down."

I picked up the receiver and heard a familiar voice. "Hi, this is Judy. I wonder if you would mind lowering the volume on the television. It's a bit loud, don't you think?"

"I'm sorry, Judy, the guys are watching a football game. I'll tell them to turn it down a few notches. Thanks for calling," I added.

Clunk!

I waved the receiver in the air and said, "I guess she hung up."

Mark chuckled and said, "What were you expecting?"

It went on and on: a need to control our television, our yard, our weeds, our garbage cans, and the type of flowers we planted in the front yard. Not having a green thumb, I was just thankful that weeds prospered in our backyard — at least they added a little green to the dry patches on the lawn.

When Judy's daughter was born, I tried to take her something special — a pink rosebud outfit with matching socks and booties. Judy thanked me but mentioned that she already had something similar and asked for the receipt so she could exchange them!

Tears clouded my eyes as I rummaged through the garbage to find the sales receipt.

While sifting through coffee grounds and orange peels, I thought, *What am I doing wrong? Even when I try to be nice, she still resists my efforts. That's it . . . no more!*

That evening, Mark put his arms around me and whispered, "It's not you, honey. Don't you realize that Judy has to be in control, and when she's not, she goes off on her tirades? You're not the problem. Just let her be!"

One year passed, then two . . . the same problems continued. One sunny afternoon in late April, I saw Judy take her daughter for a walk in the stroller and asked if I could join them.

"Oh sure," Judy replied. "C'mon, we're just going around the block."

I grabbed my sneakers and raced to catch up with them. As we walked, I listened. Judy was twenty-six years old and her parents had just moved away. She and her husband were having difficulties and Judy poured her heart out. I told her that she would be in my prayers, and if she needed anything, I would be available to listen.

Our walks became more frequent and so did the listening, which was difficult — at first — because I'm usually the talker. But the more I listened, the more I realized how much Judy needed to hear words of praise and affirmation. She was, in her own words, "always doing something wrong."

I came to realize what Judy needed more than anything else was unconditional love — not only from her family but from friends and neighbors as well.

When I asked if Judy had someone she could talk to on a regular basis, she mentioned that she and her husband, John, attended a small Bible study group. But often they couldn't go because it interfered with their daughter's sleep schedule.

Ah-ha! That was it . . . I can help, I thought.

"No problem, I'll baby-sit Jennifer while you're at the Bible study. I think it's important for both of you; I would love to help you out," I offered.

The look of shock on Judy's face mingled with an expression of genuine thankfulness was the best gift of all. Tears filled her eyes. "I can't thank you enough. That is so kind of you!" she responded.

Every Wednesday I sat with Jennifer while Judy and John had a night out and some much-needed time together with other couples their own age.

In fact, I looked forward to Wednesday nights, caring for the "granddaughter" I never had. Weeks turned into months, and Judy was so overcome with my kindness she often thanked me with more tears of appreciation.

Judy's heart began to soften, as did mine. The comments about our front yard not being color-coordinated ceased. The trash cans didn't have to be lined up perfectly all the time. And the backyard weeds didn't automatically have to be cut back to coincide with Judy's planting schedule. Judy was becoming flexible in her attitude and more patient with us as neighbors. Progress had occurred in both of our lives.

A bond of friendship grew. Judy became the daughter I never had. I loved spending time with her — frequently taking her to lunch and enjoying many afternoon walks together. My heart ached for this struggling young mom.

When my husband was hurt in an accident and came home from the hospital, Judy was ready with meals for breakfast, lunch, and dinner — not just once but three times. "I'm here to help," she whispered, while Mark slept on the sofa. "You let me know if you need anything."

"Thanks, Judy," I said. "You don't know how much that means to me." Her face beamed when I told her how much we enjoyed all of her meals — especially the baked blueberry oatmeal she brought over for breakfast that morning. Tears streamed down her cheeks. "No one has ever told me that I'm a good cook," she replied. I hugged her and said, "Not good — you're the best!"

Out of the former "weeds" from our garden have grown beautiful blossoms of love and friendship. It took time to cultivate those seeds, but today we are enjoying the fruits of our labor. We have forged a new road of neighborly love on Blossom Trail.

— Connie Pombo

When someone resists our attempts to show that we care, we can become pretty discouraged. But when Connie fell flat with her neighbor, her husband gave her wise words: "You're not the problem."

People who are tough to love are often tough to love for a reason! Sometimes, like Judy, they feel compelled to control their worlds. Sometimes they just don't know how to relate to other people. Sometimes they just don't understand what makes others tick.

When we realize we're not the problem in a relationship, it frees us. It lets us look beyond ourselves and keep trying to build a bridge without thinking we're the one who's doing something wrong.

When, like Connie, we keep reaching out in friendship, keep trying to break through, keep

trying to understand and find niches of service . . . eventually we usually do break
through to the hard-to-love person's heart.

And like Connie, we might even find a friend
who becomes as near and dear to us as our
own child. Persistence in love knits hearts
together.

LOVE'S DOORWAY

Love came cradled through my doorway, wrapped in baby-soft blankets. Sky blue eyes smiled at me from a tiny face framed in strawberry blond curls. Cory's frail body was much too small for a five-month-old. A drug-affected baby, he could not keep milk down, although he guzzled each bottle as if it were his last. He could not relax his muscles, so his tiny legs drew up tight against his chest.

When other babies his age took their first steps, Cory struggled to sit up. With time and care I watched him strengthen and grow. A year later, how I rejoiced when he held up his chubby arms, giggling as he waited for me to tickle his armpits. Laughter filled his days.

At two years old, a judge declared Cory my own little boy, legally sealing what had already taken place in my heart. Thirty years have passed and mental illness has stolen the laughter. Even so, with quiet determination Cory meets each day's challenges, gracing my life with the gift of his love and sweet spirit.

While Cory's body has grown strong with the passing years, mine has weakened. As he fights constant mental pain, I live with chronic physical pain. His perseverance teaches me how to take life's lemons and make lemonade. His loving phone calls and words of encouragement inspire me in spite of my suffering.

Love blew through my doorway, an eight-year-old whirlwind of energy and expectation. The first princess added to our family had seen far too much in her short life, making her wise beyond her years. Renee caught me off guard on our first day together. Her brown eyes sparkled with curiosity when she asked me if I was married to the dad who lives here.

I knew I was in for a roller-coaster ride of joy and pain. Renee's multiple moves through foster and adoptive homes had not crushed her zest for life. Broken promises of a forever family had not destroyed her hope that in this new home her dream would come true.

After another two years, on Valentine's Day, the judge pronounced this adorable sweetheart as my little girl. Now, twenty-eight years later, Renee still teaches me what it means not to quit in the midst of adversity.

Even as an adult, her sense of humor shines, sometimes more than I'm comfortable with. She's still likely to roll down the car window and tell the driver in the next car, "My mom thinks you're cute!" Never mind that she would die if this mom ever flirted with anyone but her daddy. I am a stronger woman because she has chosen to love me. Just thinking of my amazing daughter makes me smile.

Love tiptoed through my doorway, her trembling hands clutching her coat. Another beautiful princess, whose eight years had experienced far too much pain, melted my heart with her cautious smile. Her need to please me at every turn revealed a child driven to perform, fearful of the blows she might receive if she didn't measure up.

How strange I must have sounded to other parents when I expressed joy over my "perfect" child misbehaving. Tyana's version of acting up was laughable, but I still felt like throwing a party when she trusted me enough to assert her needs.

In seventh grade my "timid" daughter arm-wrestled all the junior high boys to the mat. After another two-year period, once again my heart sang when Tyana officially became my daughter. And now, through the twenty-four years since she captured my heart, this brave young woman has wrestled her fears to the mat — and won. She has loved me through my own insecurities and shown me what it means to fight the good fight.

The love of this beautiful "child" breathes wind into my sails, keeping me on course toward a hope-filled future. She nudges me on to achieve my dreams when I become tired and want to dock at the nearest port and stay there.

Love loped through my doorway, carrying his one bag of earthly belongings. How can eleven years have passed since Bobby's shy ten-year-old grin let me know I was a goner? He has refused to allow the first ten years of his life, mostly lived in isolation, to define him. The once insecure boy who had panic attacks over doing his homework made me proud when as a seventeen-year-old Royal Ranger he received the equivalent of Eagle Scout through our church program for young boys and teens.

As he matures into a young man, he will blaze a path for younger people whose lives were crushed. Bobby's loving words show me that he understands what it takes to be a "real" man. He is not ashamed to wrap his arms around his mom and give me a big hug, even with his buddies around.

My heart skipped a beat when a long-awaited envelope finally arrived in my mailbox with The Department of Vital Statistics written in the upper left-hand corner. I pulled out Bobby's new birth certificate that rewrote his life — and mine.

The months that followed melded into years when one day this dear son called me *Mom.* I knew he had given me a priceless gift, worth more than any riches this world can offer. His walk through continued emotional suffering reminds me that his love for me has come at great cost. Yet his heart remains soft, willing to risk loving still.

Four times now, adoption's call has knocked at my door. With each precious arrival, I have discovered new depths of love. Together, we've repeatedly visited the valleys of sorrow over separation from birth family. I've learned to release each child to love his or her birth parents, remembering that even with an abusive parent happy times happened.

Even as my wonderful birth children, Eddy, Jim, and Larry, gave me the freedom to love each new sibling, I've learned that love means letting go; I need not be the only object of my adopted children's affection. Just as my heart has grown to love each adopted child, their hearts have expanded to embrace me, while still loving those who gave them life.

On the other side of each valley, I've scaled the heights of joy to see my adopted children realize their infinite worth in simply being who they are. Their painful pasts, although never forgotten, no longer determine their futures. As I see these special children move beyond heart-wrenching memories, I witness the power of love to restore and make all things new.

Adoption's door swings wide both ways — love given and love received. Joys and sorrows shared, offering a hope and a future for them — and for me.

— *Nora Peacock*

Love is an act of faith. Nora didn't know how her relationships with her adoptive children would turn out when they first walked through her door. But she loved, in faith, trusting that she could make a difference.

Nora's birth children could have been intimidated by the new people who were entering their family. But they chose to act in faith, to love and accept the children God brought their

way. They chose to trust their parents' love —
that their parents would not lose sight of them
in the midst of the new relationships.

And entering through a new doorway into
love was an act of faith for Bobby, Tyana,
Renee, and Cory. For some of them, being
willing to love again was a big emotional risk.

Nora found her faith well placed. Through
opening her heart to new love, she says she
scaled new heights in life.

And as you love in faith, you'll scale new
heights, too.

ABOUT THE CONTRIBUTORS

Gena Bradford — writer, speaker, and singer — has published in several anthologies, periodicals, and recordings. Her latest CD, *Given Wings,* can be found at her website: *www.genabradford.com.*

Laura L. Bradford is a semi-retired caregiver who enjoys encouraging others by telling stories about faith and family.

Steven L. Brown is a cardiologist, clinical associate professor of medicine, speaker, and author of *Navigating the Medical Maze.* He lives with his wife and three children in Midland, Texas (*www.drstevenbrown.org*).

Sandy Cathcart is a freelance writer, photographer, and artist who thrives on a spirit of adventure and lives in southern Oregon. She and her husband, Cat, cook and guide for 4E Guide and Supply, a wilderness outfitter (*www.sandycathcart.com*).

Amy Chanan lives in the Denver metro area with her husband and two children. She enjoys running, hiking, and spending time with her family. She is a member of Words for the Journey Christian Writers Guild.

Doris E. Clark is the mother of three and grandmother of eight. A member of Oregon Christian Writers, Doris has written devotions, articles, and stories for magazines and compilation books.

Katherine J. Crawford and Gary, her husband of forty-nine years, reside in Omaha, Nebraska. Known as the lion-hearted Kat, you can find a snippet of her life at *www.katcrawford.com.*

Billy Cuchens and his wife, Laurie, adopted their son when he was a toddler and adopted their daughter at birth. You can read Billy's articles on topics ranging from infertility to parenting on his blog, *www.goggycoffee.blogspot.com.*

Betty J. Johnson Dalrymple lives in Parker, Colorado, where she spends time with Bob, and three children and ten grandchildren. When not enjoying traveling, she serves as liturgist for her church and facilitates a grief support group.

Midge DeSart is a wife, mother, and grandmother. Besides being author of

Maintaining Balance in a Stress-Filled World, she is a church musician and a beading embellishment artist. She and her husband live in Tacoma, Washington.

Jennifer Devlin is the author of *Life Principles for Christ-Like Living* and the *Verses We Know by Heart* study series. Visit her website, *www.ministryforlife.com,* for more information about her speaking, writing, and ministry work around the world.

Elsi Dodge is a single, retired teacher, traveling with her dog and cat in a thirty-foot RV. She lives in Boulder, Colorado. You can read her thoughts on her blog: *www.RVTourist.com/blog.*

Pamela Dowd has been a private school principal, preschool director, kindergarten teacher, legal secretary, children's clothing designer, freelance writer, and novelist. On street or treadmill she enjoys reading and walking simultaneously!

Loretta J. Eidson is author of an inspirational poetry book titled *Good Old Spiritual Food.* Her articles have appeared in the International Pentecostal Holiness (IPHC) *Experience* magazine and *Faith Café* adult curriculum.

Sheila Farmer is a homemaker and freelance writer who lives near Annapolis,

Maryland, where she is a columnist for the *Maryland Gazette*. She says, "I am ever inspired and blessed by my husband, Marvin Farmer Jr., and our two children, Shawn and Shannon."

Nancy J. Farrier is the author of twelve books and numerous articles and short stories. She has five children and one grandson, and lives in Southern California.

Louise D. Flanders worked for ten years as a procedures writer and now enjoys writing magazine articles and devotionals. She is the current secretary of the Christian Authors Guild (CAG).

Having survived a flood, a tornado that snatched her house while she and her son were in the basement, and Hurricane Katrina, **Rebecca Willman Gernon** believes if you can't find something to laugh about in every situation, you're taking life too seriously. She's currently waiting for a plague of locusts or a volcanic eruption to complete her disaster experiences.

Laquita Havens has been married to Bruce for forty-three years. A mom and grandmother, she loves to teach children through the art of storytelling and has written, directed, and produced puppet events for thirty years.

Sarah B. Hawkins teaches English and Bible to junior high students. For years she has taught a Bible study to women and has written a collection of her devotions for wives. She lives in Northern California with her husband and son.

Jon Hopkins is a youth pastor in Kansas and teaches middle school at a Christian school. He has been married for twenty-eight years and plays the mandolin (*www.thelong-aimedblow.blogspot.com*).

Sudha Khristmukti teaches English in India and writes for Christian magazines and secular newspapers. She loves playing the Sitar, listening to Western music, and rescuing stray dogs. She also has a pet squirrel and pet crow.

Kevin Lucia is a full-time English teacher and part-time graduate student. He's a staff blogger for *The Relief Journal* (*www.reliefjournal.com*), and writes a weekly column for his city newspaper, *The Press & Sun Bulletin.*

Christine McNamara is a biblical counselor and teacher who enjoys developing resources to encourage and equip others. Her work includes a training manual for mentors to previously incarcerated men and women and a support group workbook.

Emily Osburne teaches marriage workshops in the greater Atlanta area, focusing on engaged and young married couples. She wrote her first book, *Everyday Experts on Marriage,* in 2006.

Leslie J. Payne and her handsome knight enjoy travel, family, and sailing on the Chesapeake Bay. She continues to treat her chronic pain. She appreciates all she has learned through pain but hopes the relationship will one day end.

Nora Peacock, married forty years to Arlen, seldom complains about boredom. Mother of seven delightful peachicks, she brings to her writing a kaleidoscope of experiences from thirty-nine years of parenting her birth children, adopted children, and foster children.

Laurie A. Perkins lives with husband, Philip, in Needham, Massachusetts. A former children's librarian, she not only writes but also dances with the expressive worship team of Aldersgate Renewal Ministries.

Connie Pombo is an author, speaker, and founder of Women's Mentoring Ministries in Mt. Joy, Pennsylvania. When not speaking or writing, Connie enjoys photography

— one of her greatest passions (*www.conniepombo.com*).

Eileen Roddy was born in Ireland but now lives with her husband, Don Phillips, in Lawrence, Kansas. She writes a weekly column and other articles on a regular basis.

Barbara L. Scott (author of *From Rubble to Restoration*) and her husband are international ambassadors for YWAM. Barbara's passion is to use her writing and ministry to encourage others to experience God's ability to work all things together for good in their lives.

Nancy Page Sheek lives in Columbus, Georgia, with her husband, three children, and three dogs. She enjoys writing, running, traveling, and hanging out with her family. Nancy has a passion to help set women free from perfectionism and performance.

Donna Smith is a retired classroom teacher who edits and publishes the e-zine *Victory Herald* (*www.victoryherald.com*). Her works have appeared in *Guideposts, Sixth Serving of Chicken Soup for the Soul,* and *Bible Advocate.*

Jacquelyn Sandifer Strange is a retired English professor who has won awards in short story, poetry, and essay categories. She and her husband have five children and six grandchildren and have taught Sunday school for many years.

An escapee from the corporate world, **Susan Stanley** is now a full-time wife to husband Trent and mom to her two children. She writes during the children's nap times and at night.

Ann Varnum is hostess of *The Ann Varnum Show* and *Sunday Morning with Ann Varnum* on WTVY-TV, a CBS affiliate in Dothan, Alabama. Ann does a devotional series on WAQG radio (American Family Network) and for *The Dothan Eagle.*

Tamara Vermeer lives in Colorado with her husband and three children. Besides writing stories and devotions, she is an avid reader who loves to reach women through Bible studies, writing, and just listening over coffee.

Faith Waters is an itinerant elder in the African Methodist Episcopal Church. With her M.Div. in pastoral counseling, she has served as a chaplain at a youth detention center, as a youth consultant, and is a child behavioral therapist.

Chris Wright was born in England, has written thirty books, and is senior editor for a small Christian publisher in Minnesota. He has three grown children.

ABOUT THE AUTHOR

Since 1979, **Gary Chapman** has written more than twenty books. His book *The Five Love Languages* has sold five million copies in English alone and has been translated into thirty-six languages, including Arabic and Hindi. He has his own daily radio program, called *A Love Language Minute,* that can be heard on more than 100 radio stations across the United States.

In addition to his busy writing and seminar schedule, Gary Chapman is a senior associate pastor at Calvary Baptist Church in Winston-Salem, North Carolina, where he has served for thirty-six years. Gary and his wife, Karolyn, have been married for forty-five years and have two adult children and two grandchildren.

The employees of Thorndike Press hope you have enjoyed this Large Print book. All our Thorndike, Wheeler, and Kennebec Large Print titles are designed for easy reading, and all our books are made to last. Other Thorndike Press Large Print books are available at your library, through selected bookstores, or directly from us.

For information about titles, please call:
(800) 223-1244

or visit our Web site at:
http://gale.cengage.com/thorndike

To share your comments, please write:
Publisher
Thorndike Press
295 Kennedy Memorial Drive
Waterville, ME 04901